Magdalen Stuart (Maud Pember Reeves), a New Zealander, came to London in 1896 with her husband William Pember Reeves, Agent General for the New Zealand Government. Social reformer and feminist, she served untiringly for many years on the Executive Committees of the Women's Trade Union League, National Anti-Sweating League, the Central Committee for Women's Suffrage. In particular she was on the committee of the Fabian Society from 1907, serving with George Bernard Shaw, H. G. Wells, Beatrice and Sidney Webb and many other notable members of that society. In 1908 the Fabian Women's Group was founded at her London home. Having previously campaigned successfully for the implementation of women's suffrage in New Zealand, she was especially responsible for bringing the weight of the Fabian Society behind the same cause in England.

Maud Pember Reeves was appointed Director of the Educational and Propaganda Department of the Ministry of Food in the First World War. She had three children – Amber, Beryl and Fabian – and she died in 1953.

VIRAGO
is a feminist publishing company:

'It is only when women start to organize
in large numbers that we become a
political force, and begin to move towards
the possibility of a truly democratic society
in which every human being can be brave,
responsible, thinking and diligent in the struggle
to live at once freely and unselfishly'

SHEILA ROWBOTHAM
Women, Resistance and Revolution

VIRAGO
Advisory Group

ROUND ABOUT
A POUND A WEEK

BY

MRS. PEMBER REEVES

INTRODUCTION BY
SALLY ALEXANDER

Virago
London

To
My fellow worker
E.C.L.

Published by VIRAGO Limited 1979
5 Wardour Street, London W1V 3HE

First published 1913 by G. Bell & Sons Limited
Copyright © 1913 Mrs Pember Reeves

Introduction copyright © 1979 Sally Alexander

ISBN 0 86068 066 5

Virago Reprint Library No. 7

Printed in Great Britain by litho at
The Anchor Press Ltd, Tiptree, Essex

PREFACE

I AM glad to take this opportunity to acknowledge the use I have made of a manuscript written by Mrs. Charlotte Wilson, Hon. Secretary of the Fabian Women's Group. The manuscript was founded on a lecture, entitled "The Economic Disintegration of the Family," delivered by Mrs. Wilson to the Fabian Society in June, 1909. Not only ideas contained in the lecture, but also some of the wording of the manuscript, have been used in the last two chapters.

I wish also to thank Dr. Ethel Bentham for the invaluable professional service rendered by her during the five years of the investigation.

M. S. REEVES.

CONTENTS

INTRODUCTION

"How does a working man's wife bring up a family on 20s a week?" *Round About a Pound a Week* made a remarkable impact when it was first published. For four years, from 1909–1913, Maud Pember Reeves and other members of the Fabian Women's Group recorded the daily budgets and daily lives of working-class families in Lambeth. The people whose lives formed the subject of the book were by no means the poorest people in the district—the men "respectable, in full work, at a more or less top wage, young, with families still increasing". Their wives were described as "quiet, decent, 'keeping themselves to themselves' kind of women". The book came out at a time when the discussion of infant health, infant mortality and the health of mothers was dominated by the eugenicist rhetoric of race degeneration. Thinking of ways to improve the nation through "improving" the mother had become almost a national pastime. But Maud Pember Reeves' intensely moving and readable account of working-class mothers in Lambeth showed them to be at once independent, resourceful, hardworking, respectable—and very poor, bringing up their families on wholly inadequate incomes.

The national preoccupation with motherhood had its roots in the waning of national economic confidence. Since the last decades of the 19th century, under the pressure of German and American industrial competition, Britain had begun to feel its vulnerability as a world-dominating economic power. The declining birth rate and the high rate of infant mortality had taken on a new significance in the wake of the disastrous Boer War. Anxiety provoked by the physical debility of the

army recruits had been confirmed by the poverty surveys
(Charles Booth in London in the 1890s discovered 30 per cent
of the population to be living below the poverty line; Rowntree in York uncovered similar proportions). It was because of
this anxiety that the governing class acquiesced to the social
reforms of the Liberal Government of 1906 (old age pensions,
provision of school meals and school medical inspection). And
the duty of women to fulfil their natural function of motherhood efficiently and effectively became the predominant theme
of much contemporary literature. Few public figures were un-
affected by the idea that mothers were somehow responsible
for the essential wellbeing of the nation. John Burns, for
instance, a former trade unionist, President of the Local
Government Board, made the well-known statement at the
first National Conference of Infant Mortality in 1906:

> At the bottom of infant mortality, high or low, is good or bad
> motherhood. Give us good motherhood, and good pre-natal
> conditions, and I have no despair for the future of this or any
> other country.

Within the socialist movement were many individuals who
showed great concern for working-class health and many
organisations which aimed to overcome the evil effects of
poverty on the working-class mother (Margaret Macmillan's
Mother and Infant Welfare Clinic in Bradford, for instance).
But Maud Pember Reeves and the Fabian Women's Group
were unique in investigating the *daily* circumstances of
women's lives, how they coped with continual damp, vermin,
inadequate food, how they washed, cooked, scrimped for
furniture and clothes, saved for the frequent burials. The book
was based on the Fabian Women's Group investigation into
the effects on mother and child of insufficient nourishment
before and after birth, begun after registering the simple fact
that more children grew up undernourished in working-class
districts than in the wealthy districts of London such as
Kensington or Hampstead. In telling of these lives—of births,
marriages, and deaths, of ill-paid work for men and unending
toil for women, Maud Pember Reeves presented to a largely

ignorant public the realities of poverty. The conclusions were inescapable—the cause of infant mortality was not that mothers were ignorant or degenerate, but that they had too little money to provide for their own and their families' essential needs; that they lacked decent housing, domestic equipment, adequate food and clothing, and any facilities or opportunities for recreation.

By describing the experience of the poor to a primarily conventional middle-class audience, Maud Pember Reeves was revealing a world glimpsed only—if at all—through the literature and activities of philanthropy. She paid attention, therefore, to all the time-honoured shibboleths of philanthropic thought. She describes with wry humour the reason why the "gospel of porridge" was not well received at the breakfast tables of Lambeth; why thrift, cleanliness and order were not the most desirable qualities in an overworked wife and mother; and she makes short shrift of the argument that only the provident should marry and have children. If the poor were not improvident, she declares, "they would hardly dare to live their lives at all".

All this was to convince the intelligent and liberal middle classes that only the State could remedy such a situation. It was Beatrice Webb who gave the most convincing explanation for the "demand for State intervention from a generation reared amidst rapidly rising riches" when describing her own political development in *My Apprenticeship*:

> The origin of the ferment is to be discovered in a new consciousness of sin among men of intellect and men of property . . . The consciousness of sin was a collective or class consciousness; a growing uneasiness, amounting to conviction, that the industrial organisation, which had yielded rent, interest and profits on a stupendous scale, had failed to provide a decent livelihood and tolerable conditions for a majority of the inhabitants of Great Britain.

This "consciousness of sin" was bound to take very strong root in the minds of women of the middle clases in the 1880s, since whatever restrictions on economic and sexual activity masculine authority might impose, charitable work ("poor peopling" as Florence Nightingale disparagingly called it) was a legitimate activity for even the most sheltered girl in the Victorian period. As Ray Strachey has suggested in her excellent history of the feminist movement, *The Cause*, these middle-class women were moving on from dealing with the individual cases of hardship to solving the social problem. Becoming a socialist was often a consequence of that process. Autobiographies of socialist feminists show the importance of *seeing* the slums, the way in which the working class lived, in the process of conversion to socialism. Doubtless many Fabian women shared the background of one in search of "social-secretarial or organisational work" who advertised her skills in the *Fabian News*; "University Education. Experience London Settlement, Charitable Organization Society and Girls' Club." It was a short step from all these worthy organisations to membership of the Fabian Society.

It was from the Fabian Society that Maud Pember Reeves drew her distinctive brand of socialism. The society had been founded in 1844 (the name derived from the Roman general Fabius Cunctator whose tactics in his campaign against Hannibal were said to be "cautious and forthright"). Some of its more famous early members included George Bernard Shaw, Beatrice and Sidney Webb, H. G. Wells, Graham Wallas, Hubert Bland, Edith Nesbit, Annie Besant. From its inception it had always included a large number of women in its membership. Fabian socialism—a hybrid of the social conscience, often with strong evangelical roots, of the well-off and well-educated on the one hand and the pragmatism of the new professional strata (civil servants, teachers, journalists) on the other—was essentially a belief in the gradual extension of the State. The Fabians did not acknowledge the necessity of class struggle. As social democrats they simply shared rather vaguely "a common conviction of the necessity of vesting the organisation of industry and the material production in a State identified with the whole people by complete Democracy" (Preface to *Fabian Essays*, 1909). Class antagonisms could be side-stepped by the permeation of the middle and upper classes (and in particular their political and

economic institutions) with "collectivist" ideas. Thus Maud
Pember Reeves suggests in *Round About A Pound A Week* that
the State "as co-guardian of the child" must strip off "the
uniform of a police constable with a warrant in his pocket"
and "place all the information, all the security, all the help at
its command at the service of its co-guardians, the fathers and
mothers." (p 226)

Fabian women were content to remain quietly inside the
Fabian society, representing a fairly large proportion of its
membership (between a quarter and a third) until 1908, when,
according to the pamphlet *Three Years of Work*, the period of
militant suffragist agitation produced:

> . . . unrest among women within the Fabian Society as well as
> outside. The socialist movement was rapidly growing in volume
> and force, and encountering increasingly bitter opposition, and
> many ardent suffragists amongst the Fabian women felt that the
> society was not keeping pace with a movement to which it
> recently committed itself by the inclusion of a new Clause in its
> basis. [A statement of equal rights for women.]

In 1908, Charlotte Wilson, an anarchist and one of the
earliest member of the Fabian Society, founded the Fabian
Women's Group at the London home of Maud Pember
Reeves, and in the following year the "Mother Allowance
Scheme in Lambeth"—as the project was called which was
later to become *Round About A Pound A Week*—was begun on
the initiative of Maud Pember Reeves. According to her
daughter, Amber Blanco White, no sooner had the idea
occurred to her mother than she set to work on it, enlisting
the help of her sister Mrs Lascelles, who had lived with the
Pember Reeves family since her husband's death, and Dr
Ethel Bentham. They set up a sub-committee in the Group
for their work, and Charlotte Wilson became the Treasurer of
the project, contributing the two final chapters of the book.

The focus on the working-class wife and mother was not the
personal whim of Maud Pember Reeves. It expressed the
political ideas of Fabian feminism. The imprint of Fabian
socialism on *Round About A Pound A Week* lay in the concern

with poverty, the extension of the State; but the emphasis on the houseworker and mother came from feminism.

In fact the ideas coming out of the Fabian Women's Group at this time offer wider understanding of the activities of social-ist feminists at a time when the dominating struggle was the agitation for women's suffrage. Numbering only 230 at its peak in 1912, the group concentrated on women's social welfare and political rights, and their contribution to reform was important and influential. From a separate office in Tothill Street, Westminster, they published numerous pamphlets, tracts and two highly praised books, of which *Round About A Pound A Week* is one. Although less active in the inter-war period, the Fabian Women's Group enjoyed a brief renaissance after 1938 with the re-organisation of the Fabian Society and until the Group's end in 1952. Among its other members were Charlotte Payne Townshend (Mrs Bernard Shaw), Dr Letitia Fairfield, Beatrice Webb, Marion Phillips, Margaret Bondfield, Susan Lawrence and in later years Barbara Drake, Frida Laski and Margaret Cole.

The two immediate aims of the Fabian Women's Group were equality in citizenship and women's economic in-dependence. The first was prompted by a suggestion from Beatrice Webb that "in local government women's citizenship is theoretically recognised but imperfect—ill understood, un-appreciated and little used, whilst the evils crying out for women's intervention are enormous." The Group set out to rectify this with characteristic energy. A sub-committee was formed, and money raised. 10 women were deputed to investigate local bodies in their areas on which women could sit, or with which they might work. They tackled the edu-cation of 100,000 women within the London County Council boundaries, to enable them to get the necessary qualifications for becoming electors. Their policies resulted in Fabian women being elected to Poor Law Boards, and occasionally to local councils; they served as school managers, on care committees and in local government associations. Fabian women were also among the militant suffragists. Several members were imprisoned and underwent forced feeding (experiences which characteristically produced a sub-committee and eventually a pamphlet). And there was no sectarianism within the Group: its members belonged to nearly the whole range of suffrage societies, and indeed to other socialist parties, notably the Women's Labour League (Dr Marion Phillips for instance, and Ethel Bentham) and the Independent Labour Party (Ethel Bentham, Margaret Bondfield, Mary Macarthur).

But the distinctive quality of Fabian feminism in this period was its economic individualism. The first aim of the Fabian Women's Group (it was often re-worded) was declared in 1913 to be: "To study the economic position of women and press their claim to equality with men in the personal economic independence to be secured by socialism." Socialism was to provide complete economic independence for women by three means. Firstly, the full and equal participation of women in paid work; secondly, the training of skilled domestic workers and/or the provision of co-operative households; and thirdly, some form of State support for maternity and costs of child-rearing, i.e. the "State Endowment of Motherhood". (The Women's Co-operative Guild, an organisation very largely of working-class housewives, was even more comprehensive in its schemes for maternity and childcare. See *Maternity: Letters from Working Women,* edited M. L. Davies.)

The emphasis on economic independence explains why Maud Pember Reeves was so critical of the notion of the "family wage". Not that such a wage existed, but in a talk she gave on socialism and women, she stated:

> The family must not be the economic unit. We talk of a wage of 20s., or 30s., or 35s., as a family wage, paid to one wage earner, quite irrespective of his family.

The elimination of the idea of the family wage and the disintegration of the family as the economic unit of society were ideas based on an historical analysis of the position of women which is still much in evidence today. It was argued by these women that the industrial revolution had removed industry from the home, forcing working-class women into poorly paid factory work, and reducing middle-class women to "parasitism"—economically dependent on their fathers and husbands, deprived of productive work, diminished in human dignity. This analysis, cogently presented by Mabel Atkinson in *The Economic Foundations of the Women's Movement* (Fabian Tract No. 175) is interesting because, by distinguishing the effects of the industrial revolution on the two main classes of women, it separated the demands of middle-class and working-class women, and explained their different consciousness:

> So, at the present time, there are two main sections in the modern women's movement – the movement of the middle-class women who are revolting against their exclusion from human activity and insisting, firstly, on their right to education, which is now practically conceded on all sides; secondly, on their right to earn a livelihood for themselves, which is rapidly being won; and thirdly, on their right to share in the control of Government, the point around which the fight is now most fiercely raging. These women are primarily rebelling against the sex-exclusiveness of men, and regard independence and the right to work as the most valuable privilege to be striven for.
>
> On the other hand, there are the women of the working classes, who have been faced with a totally different problem and who naturally react in a different way . . . What the woman of the proletariat feels as her grievance is that her work is too long and too monotonous, the burden laid upon her is too heavy. Moreover, in her case that burden is due to the power of capitalistic exploitation resulting from the injustice of our social system. It is not due . . . to the fact that the men of her class shut her out from gainful occupation. Therefore among the working class women there is less sex consciousness . . . The reforms that she demands are not independence and the right to work, but rather protection against the unending burden of toil which has been laid upon her. (p 15)

Yet, in spite of the different immediate concerns of women in the two classes, the Fabian women felt that their ultimate objective must be the same: the achievement of economic independence. Even more, they felt that industrial capitalism itself was forcing the two groups together—middle-class women into realising that emancipation didn't lie in wage

labour as it was then organised, working-class women into
recognising the suffering that "parasitism" brought, and that
their interests were not always represented by those of working
men.

The Fabian women recognised that State intervention in
women's lives through the Factory Acts was made necessary
by excessive exploitation of women workers in the new
industrial conditions. Thus the precedent was set for the State
as "guardian" of women (and children). (This point was
always raised by Mary Macarthur, founder of the National
Federation of Women Workers, when discussing the problems
of organising women workers. She remarked that historically
it had always been easier for women to improve their conditions of work through protective legislation from the State
than through self-organisation.) The State must step in to put
an end to women's economic dependence, firstly through the
establishment of a legal minimum wage, and secondly through
the "State Endowment of Motherhood".

These two themes, the essential harmony of economic
interests among women from different class backgrounds, and
the emphasis on State provision for women's economic independence perhaps go part of the way towards explaining
why it was that this predominantly middle-class, relatively
privileged group of women could claim to speak on behalf of
all women and not just themselves. But there is also another
explanation.

The Fabian Women's Group was the voice of the "educated" woman. Its members were teachers, lecturers, journalists, writers, dancers, artists and the wives and daughters of
educated and professional men. Membership surveys also
reveal one or two nurses, sanitary inspectors, gardeners, civil
servants, as well as a large number of type-writers and
secretaries. Margaret Bondfield (Fabian, member of the
Independent Labour Party, shop assistant and the first woman
to sit on the General Council of the TUC), gave a talk to the
Fabian Women's Group in 1910 on "Wage-earning Mothers"
in which she determined the class position of women by their
education: women who had only been to elementary school

(compulsory state education up to the age of 14) were working class, all the rest were middle class. This distinction definitely cast most of the Fabian Women's Group into the middle class.

But Margaret Bondfield's division was a little over-simplified; there seems to have been at least two broad groups of women within the Fabian Women's Group. The first was the imposing number of intellectual and professional women. The biographies of all the leading members of the Fabian Women's Group reveal a formidable array of qualifications and achievements. Practically every woman of note in the trade union, labour or socialist movements participated in its conferences, lecture series and research projects, if they did not actually join the Group. The second group of women, and this is more speculative, came from the less elevated branches of the teaching profession, clerks, type-writers and secre-taries. There had been a burst of union activity amongst these women workers in the five years before the formation of the Fabian Women's Group. It seems probable, therefore, given the emphasis in the Fabian Women's Group on women's economic independence, that some of these younger women joined the Society.

There might have been a certain distance between the older generation of women (Beatrice Webb, Charlotte Wilson and Maud Pember Reeves, for instance), and their younger sisters. The older generation did not take their education and their hard-won professional status lightly. Their achievements had been bitterly fought for through political campaigns and agitation; some of the younger women, they thought, took these victories and the opportunities they opened up for granted. There are also faint residues of Victorian standards of propriety about some of the older women. When I asked Amber Blanco White for a description of her mother's friends in the FWG, she replied that there "was never any time to meet any of them—they were just a lot of women talking about very serious things." Her mother thought it was im-portant for girls to study their lessons most of the time: having been well educated herself, and her mother before her, she wanted her daughters to grow up in the same way. And so they did—Amber Blanco White studied philosophy at Cambridge, her sister went to the Royal College of Music. Femininity tended to be identified with frivolity—they kept a vigilant watch on this side of their character. In the 1909 annual report of the Group, women were urged to "cast aside feminine slackness and negligence with regard to their own affairs", and get on with the work of preparing for citizenship.

There was no intellectual dogmatism in the Fabian Women's Group. There were many divergent views, but the unifying theme was the fundamental acceptance of the economic basis of women's subjection. They believed they could speak for the majority of women because their analysis of sex oppression *was* economic. In spite of middle-class women's wider opportunities for education and training, all women were disadvantaged on the labour market compared to men. While the grossest forms of exploitation were suffered by working-class women, women in middle-class occupations were also struggling under the burden of low wages, lack of skills, and very often had other people to support as well as themselves. (One of the most interesting and widely quoted inquiries undertaken by the Fabian Women's Group was Ellen Smith's *Wage Earning Women and their Dependants* 1915.) And mothers in both classes were unable to support themselves or their children.

It was therefore quite undesirable that men should be paid a "family wage"—this would simply increase women's subjection to them. It was also a bad idea to send mothers out to paid work. The solution in the eyes of the Fabian women was the "State Endowment of Motherhood". The strength in their position lay in their clear conceptual distinction between women as mothers, women as wives, and women as wage earners. This meant that they could thoroughly analyse the problems and organise around them. Its weakness lay in the identification of the State with both the democratic and the national interest. The absence of a theory of class struggle and the notion that the individual could have a direct, unmediated relationship with the State, left the door wide open for all sorts of ideas equating the national interest with motherhood

and children. (Sidney Webb most notably seized on the re-
lationship between motherhood and imperialism: (see
"Imperialism and Motherhood", Anna Davin, in *History
Workshop Journal*, No. 5).

The focus on motherhood in the Fabian Women's Group
originated, however, in the desire to uncover the essential
attributes and implications of sexual difference. In this
respect they were quite unlike the more orthodox liberal or
bourgeois feminists. Millicent Garrett Fawcett, for instance,
refused to acknowledge the difference of sex. Women as wage
earners were neutered units of labour; motherhood did not
enter into her economic calculations. She was extremely
irritated when Eleanor Rathbone took over the Presidency of
the National Society for Equal Citizenship and immediately
began to campaign for the inclusion of the endowment of
motherhood in its demands. For Millicent Fawcett, the
progress of the women's movement was measured by the
"successive removal of intolerable grievances". The Fabian
women did not allow themselves such a political creed. They
wanted the re-organisation of society, the incorporation of
industry into the State, the absorption by the State of all
fundamental economic functions and processes. This, they
believed, was the road to socialism, and their motive in form-
ing the Fabian Women's Group was to ensure that women too
should determine their own fate, should define for themselves
the relationship between socialism and economic independence. Their particular analysis of the threads connecting
women's economic exploitation with sexual oppression led
them to produce pamphlets and books, to embark on numerous campaigns, contributing to the profound changes in the
relation of the State to the welfare of ordinary people over the
past decades.

In *Round About A Pound A Week*, Maud Pember Reeves was
determined to convince the intelligent and liberal middle
classes of "the glorious common sense of socialism", the
rightness of State co-operation in parenthood. But the real
strength of this most readable book lies in the detailed account
it gives of working-class women's domestic work and

household management. Maud Pember Reeves did not presume to teach poor women how to run their homes; she wanted to learn about their daily lives from their own lips. *Round About A Pound A Week* is a neglected work by an important group of women; with it, a vital piece is added to our fragmented view of working-class lives in the years before the First World War.

I should like to thank Linda Walker and the staff at Nuffield College Library for the help they gave me with the Introduction.

AUGUST 1978   SALLY ALEXANDER

ROUND ABOUT
A POUND A WEEK

CHAPTER I

THE DISTRICT

TAKE a tram from Victoria to Vauxhall Station. Get out under the railway arch which faces Vauxhall Bridge, and there you will find Kennington Lane. The railway arch roofs in a din which reduces the roar of trains continually passing overhead to a vibrating, muffled rumble. From either end of the arch comes a close procession of trams, motor-buses, brewers' drays, coal-lorries, carts filled with unspeakable material for glue factory and tannery, motor-cars, coster-barrows, and people. It is a stopping-place for tramcars and motor-buses; therefore little knots of agitated persons continually collect on both pathways, and dive between the vehicles and descending passengers in order to board the particular bus or tram they desire. At rhythmic intervals all traffic through the arch is suspended to allow a flood of trams, buses, drays, and vans, to surge and rattle and bang across the opening of the archway which faces the river.

At the opposite end there is no cross-current. The trams slide away to the right towards the Oval. In front is Kennington Lane, and to the left, at right angles, a narrow street connects with Vauxhall Walk, leading farther on into Lambeth Walk, both locally better known as The Walk. Such is the western gateway to the district stretching north to Lambeth Road, south to Lansdowne Road, and east to Walworth Road, where live the people whose lives form the subject of this book.

They are not the poorest people of the district. Far from it ! They are, putting aside the trades-men whose shops line the big thoroughfares such as Kennington Road or Kennington Park Road, some of the more enviable and settled inhabitants of this part of the world. The poorest people—the river-side casual, the workhouse in-and-out, the bar-room loafer—are anxiously ignored by these respectable persons whose work is per-manent, as permanency goes in Lambeth, and whose wages range from 18s. to 30s. a week.

They generally are somebody's labourer, mate, or handyman. Painters' labourers, plumbers' labourers, builders' handymen, dustmen's mates, printers' labourers, potters' labourers, trouncers for carmen, are common amongst them. Or they may be fish-fryers, tailors' pressers, feather-cleaners' assistants, railway-carriage washers, employees of dust contractors, carmen for Borough Council contractors, or packers of various descriptions. They are respectable men in full work, at a more or less top wage, young, with families still increasing, and they will be lucky if they are never worse off than they now are. Their wives are quiet, decent, " keep themselves-to-themselves " kind of women, and the children are the most punctual and regular scholars, the most clean-headed children of the poorer schools in Kennington and Lambeth.

The streets they live in are monotonously and drearily decent, lying back from the main arteries, and with little traffic other than a stray barrel-organ, a coal-lorry selling by the hundredweight sack, or a taxi-cab going to or from its driver's dinner at home. At certain hours in the day—before morning school, at midday, and after four o'clock—these narrow streets become full of screaming, running, shouting children. Early in the morning men come from every door and pass out of sight. At different times during the evening the same men straggle home again. At all other hours the street is quiet and desperately dull. Less ultra-respectable neighbourhoods may have a certain picturesqueness, or give a sense of community of interest or of careless comradeship, with their untidy women chatting in the doorways and their unoccupied men lounging at the street corners; but in these superior streets a kind of dull aloofness seems to be the order of the day.

The inhabitants keep themselves to themselves, and watch the doings of the other people from behind window curtains, knowing perfectly that every incoming and outgoing of their own is also jealously recorded by critical eyes up and down the street. A sympathetic stranger walking the length of one of these thoroughfares feels the atmosphere of criticism. The rent-collector, the insurance agent, the coal-man, may pass the time of day with worn women in the doorways, but a friendly smile from the stranger receives no response. A weekly caller becomes the abashed object of intense interest on the part of everybody in the street, from the curious glances of the green-grocer's lady at the corner to the appraising stare of the fat little baker who always manages to be on his doorstep across the road. And everywhere along the street is the visitor conscious of eyes which disappear from behind veiled windows. This consciousness accentuates the dispiriting outlook.

The houses are outwardly decent—two stories of grimy brick. The roadway is narrow, but on the whole well kept, and on the pavement outside many doors there is to be noticed, in a greater or less condition of freshness, a semicircle of hearth-stone, which has for its radius the length of the housewife's arm as she kneels on the step. In some streets little paved alley-ways lead behind the front row of houses, and twist and turn among still smaller dwellings at the back—dwellings where the front door leads downwards into a room instead of upwards into a passage. Districts of this kind cover dreary acres—the same little two-story house, with or without an inconceivably drearier basement, with the same kind of baker's shop at the corner faced by the same kind of greengrocer's shop opposite. The ugly, constantly-recurring school buildings are a relief to the spirit oppressed by the awful monotony.

The people who live in these places are not really more like one another than the people who live in Belgrave Square or South Kensington. But there is no mixture of rich and poor, no startling contrast, no crossing-sweeper and no super-taxpayer, and the first impression is that of uniformity. As a matter of fact, the characteristics of Mrs. Smith of Kennington and the characteristics of Mrs. Brown who lives next door are more easily to be differentiated by a stranger in the street than are the characteristics of Mrs. Smythe of Bayswater from those of Mrs. Browne who occupies the house next to her.

Mrs. Smith and Mrs. Brown, though they may never be seen by the passer-by, are able to imprint their personality on the street because their ways are open, and meant to be open, to all whom it may concern. Mrs. Smith likes red ochre at her door, in spite of the children's boots messing it all over the floor. Moreover, she likes to cover the big flagstone in front of the door, and two lesser stones, one on each side; she makes the edges coincide with the cracks, and produces a two-winged effect of deep importance. It is likely that Mrs. Smith's mother lived in a village where not to do your doorstep thus was a social sin, where perhaps there was but one flagstone, and Mrs. Smith in her childhood was accustomed to square edges.

Mrs. Brown " can't abide that nasty stuff," and uses good hearthstone, as her mother taught her to do. Mrs. Brown prefers also the semi-circular sweep of the arm which secures the rounded edge and curved effect which satisfy her sense of propriety and usualness.

Mrs. Smith has a geranium in a pot in her front window, and the lace curtains which shield her privacy behind it are starched and blued according to some severe precedent ignored by the other ladies of the neighbourhood.

Mrs. Brown goes in for a scheme of window decoration which shows the dirt less. She has a row of red and yellow cocoa tins to make a bright effect.

The merest outsider calling for the first time on Mrs. Smith knows her beforehand for the decent, cleanly soul she is, and only wonders whether the struggle of life has worn her temper to fiddle-strings or whether some optimistic strain in her nature still allows her to hope on. The same outsider looking at Mrs. Brown's front door and window would realize her to be one who puts a good face on things, and, if it happened to be the right time of a day which was not washing-day,

probably would expect, after the proper cere-
monial had been gone through, to be asked in to
sit behind the cocoa tins.

Who could tell anything half so interesting
from the front doors of Mrs. Smythe and Mrs.
Browne of Bayswater ? Who could tell, on
meeting each of these ladies face to face, more
than her official age and the probable state of her
husband's purse ?

The children of the street are equally different
from one another both in character and appearance, and are often startlingly good-looking.
They have shrill voices, clumsy clothes, the look
of being small for their age, and they are liable
to be comfortably dirty, but there the characteristics they have in common cease. They may be
wonderfully fair, with delicate skins and pale
hair; they may have red hair, with snub-nosed,
freckled faces; or they may be dark and intense,
with long, thick eyelashes and slender, lithe
bodies. Some are apathetic, some are restless.
They are often intelligent; but while some are
able to bring their intelligence to bear on their
daily life, others seem quite unable to do so. They
are abnormally noisy. Had they been well
housed, well fed, well clothed, and well tended,
from birth, what kind of raw material would
they have shown themselves to be ?

CHAPTER II

THE PEOPLE

It was this question which started an investigation which has been carried on for four years by a committee of the Fabian Women's Group. A sum of money was placed at the disposal of this committee in order to enable them to study the effect on mother and child of sufficient nourishment before and after birth. Access was obtained to the list of out-patients of a well-known lying in hospital; names and addresses of expectant mothers were taken from the list, and a couple of visitors were instructed to undertake the weekly task of seeing each woman in her own home, supplying the nourishment, and noting the effects. From as long as three months before birth, if possible, till the child was a year old, the visits were to continue. The committee decided that the wives of men receiving over 26s. a week were likely to have already sufficient nourishment, while the wives of men out of work or receiving less than 18s. a week were likely to be living in a state of such misery that the temptation to let the rest of the family share in the mother's and baby's nourishment would be too great.

They therefore only dealt with cases where the wages ranged between 18s. and 26s. a week. After two years' experience they raised the higher limit to 30s.

For the convenience of visiting it was necessary to select an area. The district described in the previous chapter was chosen because it is within reach of the weighing centre, where each infant could be brought once a fortnight to see the doctor and have its weight recorded. A member of the committee who is a doctor interviewed each woman before the visits began, in order to ascertain if her health and her family history were such that a normal baby might be expected. It was at first proposed to rule out disease, but pulmonary and respiratory disease were found to be so common that to rule them out would be to refuse about half the cases. It was therefore decided to regard such a condition of health as normal, and to refuse only such cases of active or malignant disease in the parents as might, in the doctor's opinion, completely wreck the child's chance of a healthy life.

Drink, on the other hand, the committee had expected to find a normal condition, and had proposed the acceptance of moderate drinking. Experience, however, went to prove that married men in full work who keep their job on such a wage do not and cannot drink. The 1s. 6d. or 2s. which they keep for themselves has to pay for their own clothes, perhaps fares to and from work, smoking and drinking. It does not allow much margin for drunkenness. A man whose wife declared him to be "spiteful" on Saturday nights was certainly the worse for drink on Saturday nights; but never once during sixteen months of weekly visiting did he omit to bring his wife her full allowance. He had kept his job for many years, and the explanation is that he was given tips at the theatre for which he worked. The tips he, not unnaturally, considered to be peculiarly his own.

One other man, who could make fair wages when in work, turned out thoroughly unsatisfactory. He was not a drunkard, but he would have been if he could have afforded it. Otherwise the record is fairly clear. Men who earned overtime money or who received tips might spend some of it on beer, but the regular wage was too close a fit to allow of much indulgence. Many of the men were teetotallers, and some did not even smoke.

It was found to be necessary, in order to secure the success of the investigation, to inaugurate a system of accurate accounts. In no case were these accounts already in being, and it was therefore the task of the visitors to teach each woman in turn to keep a record of her expenditure for the week. As the greater part of this volume is to do with these weekly budgets, this is a good opportunity to explain why they are credible evidence of real conditions.

A working man's wife in receipt of a regular allowance divides it as follows: Rent; burial insurance; coal and light; cleaning materials; clothing; food. A short experience in helping her to sort her items on paper shows the investigator how to prove their accuracy. Rent is easy. There is always the rent-book if the family deals direct with the landlord; and if the rooms are sublet from the real tenant, the woman who sublets them is only too anxious to explain either that rent is owing or that it is paid regularly, and how much a week it is. Burial insurance is easy. The insurance-book tells the whole story. With regard to such items as coal, gas, soap, and food, experience enables an intelligent investigator to compare accounts of women who do not know of one another's existence in such a manner as to know, almost before the woman has spoken, what she is likely to be spending. If a woman says that she is buying 1 cwt. of coal a week in the winter, and paying 1s. 6d. for it, dozens of other accounts of which she knows nothing corroborate her. If she says she is burning 1¾ cwt. in the winter, and spending 2s. 7½d., the price is known to be correct; it only remains to question the quantity. In one case the reason is that the rooms are basement rooms, very damp and very dark. In another there are eight children, with a very large copper fire to be kept going on washing-days. In a third no gas is laid on, and all the cooking has to be done by the stove. All these conditions are there to be seen. With regard to food the same test applies. Is the budget peculiar, or does it bear out thirty others, allowing, of course, for difference in size of family and in size of income ? If it is peculiar, why ? The explanation is generally simple and obvious. In cases where there is no explanation—of which there have been two only—the family is not visited any further. As a matter of fact, the budgets have borne out each other in the most striking manner. There seems to be so little choice in the manner of keeping a family on 20s. a week.

The women were with one consent appalled at the idea of keeping accounts. Not that they did not " know it in their heads," as they anxiously explained; but the clumsy writing and the difficult spelling, and the huge figures which refused to keep within any appointed bounds, and wandered at will about the page, thoroughly daunted them.

Eight women were found who could neither read nor write. They said that it was not thought of much consequence when they were girls; but they evidently found it extremely humiliating now, from the difficulty with which the acknow-ledgment of their disability was pumped out of them. Of these eight, three had husbands who undertook the task for them. The men's hand-writing was excellent, the figures and spelling clear and correct, but at first details were lamentably absent. " Groceries," even " sundries," were common entries, and, as the scribe was always away at work, the visitor was left to the mercy of bursts of memory on the part of the mother, whose anxious efforts to please at any cost might land everybody concerned in further difficulties. The only method in such cases was to make her sit down and shut her eyes, pretend the visitor was her " young man " (generic term for husband), and think it out all over again. Pencil in hand, the eager listener caught and made accounts out of such recollections as these: " 'E give me twenty-two bob a Satterday. After I put Ernie ter bed I went shoppin' in the Walk." Long pause. " I know I got 'arf a shoulder er mutton at 1s. 9d., an' 3 pounds er pertaters, and they was 1½d., an' a cabbage w'ich 'e said was as fresh as a daisy, but it turned out to be all fainty like w'en I come to cook it." When the record is taken down in proper form, it is compared with the masculine accounts. If the two agree, jubilation; if not, why not ? And we begin all over again. After a few weeks of such experiences the husband always reformed.

Other illiterate women employed an eldest child of perhaps ten or eleven years of age. In these cases a certain kind of painstaking accuracy could be relied upon, but, far from resorting to masculine short-cuts, these little secretaries usually went to the other extreme, and gave way to a prolix style, founded, doubtless, on the maternal manner of recollecting. One account, kept in large copybook hand by Emma, aged eleven, began as follows: " Mr G's wages was 19 bob out of that e took thruppons for es diner witch is not mutch e bein sutch a arty man. The rent was six and Mrs G payed fower an six because Bobby's boots was off is feet and his knew ones was one an six witch makes six and that leaves 12 an 9 and out of that," etc. It took four pages of painstaking manuscript in a school exercise-book to complete one week. This serial story had to be reduced, though with regret, to the limits of ordinary accounts.

Other young scribes had special tricks, such as turning their fractions upside down or running two or more words into one. " Leggerbeef " and " dryaddick " recurred week after week in one book, and " lberpeces " in another. The first two only had to be pronounced to solve their own riddle, but the third had to be worried through recollection after recollection till it turned out to mean " 1 lb. of pieces," or 1 lb. of scraps of meat.

The women who kept their accounts for themselves were found to be better arithmeticians than they were writers. Their addition had a disconcerting way of being correct, even when the visitor seemed to get a different total. But, then, the spelling was sometimes beyond the sharpened wits of the most experienced Fabian women to comprehend. Great care had to be taken not to hurt their feelings as they sat anxiously watching

the visitor wrestling with the ungainly collection
of words and figures. " Coull " did not mean
coal, which appeared as " coles " quite clearly
lower down. It was Lambeth for cow-heel.
" Earrins too d " meant " herrings, 2d."
" Sewuitt " is simple, more so than " suit," a
common form of " suet "; but " wudanole " and
" curince " gave some trouble. They stood for
" wood and oil " and " currants." Seeing the
visitor hesitate over the item " yearn 1d.," the
offended mother wrote next week " yearn is for
mending sokes."

Some of the women—in fact, the majority—
wrote a good hand and spelled fairly well. Those
who had before marriage been in work where
anything of the kind was expected of them—such
as that of a tea-shop waitress or of a superior
domestic servant—quickly turned into interested
and competent accountants. But the older
women, and those who had had no reason to use a
pencil after leaving school, had completely lost
the power of connecting knowledge which might
be in their minds with marks made by their hand
on a piece of paper. These women were curiously
efficient in a kind of mental arithmetic, though
utterly at sea directly pencil touched paper.
On the whole, accounts came into being sooner
than at first sight seemed possible.

The women were suspicious and reserved.
They were all legally married women, because
the hospital from whose lists their names had been

taken dealt only with married women. They con-
quered their reserve in most cases, but not in all.
Some were grateful; some were critical. At the
beginning of each case the woman seemed to steel
herself to sit patiently and bear it while the
expected questions or teaching of something
should follow. She generally appeared to be
conscious that the strange lady would probably
like to sit in a draught, and, if complimented on
her knowledge of the value of fresh air and open
windows, she might repeat in a weary manner
commonplaces on the subject which had obviously been picked up from nurse, doctor, or
sanitary inspector.

They spoke well of their husbands when they
spoke of them at all, but it is the children chiefly
who fill their lives. The woman who said, " My
young man's that good ter me I feel as if somethink
nice 'ad 'appened every time 'e comes in," was
obviously speaking the simple truth, and she was
more articulate than most of the others, whose
" 'E's all right " might mean as much. Another
woman introduced the subject as follows: " 'E's
a good 'usbin. 'E ain't never kep' back me
twenty-three bob, but 'e's that spiteful Satterday nights I 'as ter keep the children from 'im."
" And what do *you* do ?" asked the interested
visitor. " Oh, me ? That's all right. I'm
cookin' 'is supper," she explained, as though to a
child.

On the whole they seemed to expect judgment

to be passed on the absent man according to the amount he allowed them. Many were the anxious explanations when the sum was less than 20s.—that it was " all 'e got," or that " 'e only keeps one and six, an' 'e buys 'is cloes 'isself, an' 'e's teetotler an' don't 'ardly smoke at all." The idea among them, roughly speaking, seemed to be that if he allowed less than 20s. explanations were required; if 20s., nothing need be said beyond " It ain't much, but you can't grumble." If over 20s., it was rather splendid, and deserved a word of notice about once in six weeks, when it would be good manners for the visitor to say, " I see Mr. A. never fails to bring you your twenty-two," and Mrs. A. would probably answer, " 'E's all right," but would look gratified.

The homes are kept in widely different states of order, as is to be expected. There is the rigidly clean and tidy, the fairly clean and tidy, the moderately clean but very untidy. The difference depends on many factors: the number of children, the amount of money to spend, the number of rooms, the personality of the husband and the personality of the wife. Six or eight children give a great deal of work, and leave very little time in which to do it. In a family of that number there is nearly certain, besides the baby, to be an ex-baby, and even perhaps an ex-ex-baby, all at home to be looked after all day long and to create fresh disorder every minute. The amount of money to spend affects cleanliness very closely. It decides the number of rooms; it decides the amount of soap and of other cleaning materials and utensils; and it probably decides the question of water laid on or water to be carried up from the back-yard, and, when used, down again. A family of four children in one room is a problem. Two may be at school part of the day, but two will be at home all the time, and there will be no moment when the mother can put them to sleep in another room and get rid of them while she washes and cleans. Her chance of peace or method is small with the always recurring work of the dinner to cook and the utensils to wash, with the children ever present in the same room.

But the personality of the parents is, of course, the chief cause of order or disorder. A man who loves order has a great influence for order, and a man who likes to go to bed in his boots and spit on the floor has an almost overwhelming influence in the other direction. He may be an equally good fellow in all other respects, but his wife, if she has a tidy nature, may quarrel bitterly with him; whereas if she is more easy-going she may remain his good friend, through not feeling constant irritation and insult because of his ways. It is a fact that a woman the law of whose being is cleanliness and order at all costs may, to a slovenly man, make a most tiresome wife. Her little home may be shining and spotless—as far as anything can be shining and spotless in Lambeth—at the cost of all her vitality and all her temper. She herself may, as a result of her desperate battle with dirt and discouragement, be a scold and an unreasonable being. She cannot be got away from in two rooms where a light and fire can only be afforded in one, and she may be the greatest trial in an always difficult life. In such homes as £1 a week can buy in London, the women who do not insist upon doing the impossible, and fretting themselves and everybody else because it is impossible, often arrive at better results—with regard at least to the human beings about them—than the women who put furniture first and the peace of the family second. And this even if the rooms in their charge do look as though their dark places would not bear inspection. The mother who is not disturbed by a little mud on the floor has vitality left to deal with more important matters.

To manage a husband and six children in three rooms on round about £1 a week needs, first and foremost, wisdom and loving-kindness, and after that as much cleanliness and order as can be squeezed in. The case where the man loves order and the woman is careless may also be prolific of strained relations between the parents. But a steady woman who is not as tidy as her husband might wish has many ways of producing a semblance of order which makes for peace while he is there, and the friction is less likely to be intense. Of course, if both parents are orderly by nature all is well. The home will be clean, and the children will be brought up in tidy ways, much to their advantage. But if there are to be constant and bitter recriminations over the state of the house, better, for the man's sake, the children's sake, and the woman's sake, a dingy room where peace and quiet are than a spotless abode where no love is.

CHAPTER III

HOUSING

How does a working man's wife bring up a family on 20s. a week ? Assuming that there are four children, and that it costs 4s. a week to feed a child, there would be but 4s. left on which to feed both parents, and nothing at all for coal, gas, clothes, insurance, soap, or rent. Four shillings is the amount allowed the foster-mother for food in the case of a child boarded out by some Boards of Guardians; therefore it would seem to be a justifiable figure to reckon upon. But for a woman with 20s. a week to spend it is evidently ridiculously high. If the calculation were to be made upon half this sum, would it be possible ? The food for the children in that case would amount to 8s. To allow the same amount to each parent as to each child would not be an extravagance, and we should on that basis arrive at the sum of 12s. a week for the food of six people. That would leave 8s. for all other expenses. But rent alone may come to 6s. or 7s., and how could the woman on 20s. a week manage with 1s., or perhaps 2s., for coal, gas, insurance, clothes, cleaning materials, and thrift ?

The usual answer to a question of this kind is that the poor are very extravagant. It is no answer. It does not fit the question. But what matter if only it saves people from thinking ? Another answer sometimes given is that everything in districts where people are poor is cheaper, because the people are poor, than it would be in districts where people are rich. Now, is that so ? If it were, it might in some degree help to solve the problem.

To take the item of rent:—a single room in Lambeth, 15 feet by 12 feet, upstairs, with two windows—a good room—costs a poor man 4s. a week. A house containing eighteen rooms in South Kensington, for rent, rates, and taxes, may cost a rich man £250 a year. If the rich man were to pay 4s. a week for every 20 square yards of his floor space, he would pay, not £250 a year, but £285. If he were to pay 4s. a week for the same amount of cubic space for which the Lambeth man is paying his 4s., he would pay, not £250 a year, but £500. Added to which he gets an elaborate system of water laid on (hot and cold), baths, waste pipes and sinks from top to bottom of the house. He also gets an amount of coal-cellarage which enables him to buy his coal cheap, and he gets good air and light and space round his house, so that he can keep his doctor's bills down. He certainly has a better bargain for his £250 a year than the poor man has for his 4s. a week. Therefore it is not true to say that a family can be brought up on 20s. a week in Lambeth because a poor man can make a better bargain over his rent than can a rich man. As a matter of fact, we see that he actually pays more per cubic foot of space than the rich man does.

A comparison might be made in something like the following way :

A middle-class well-to-do man with income of £2,000	might pay in rent, rates, and taxes, £250—	a proportion of his income which is equal to *one-eighth.*
A middle-class comfortable man, with income of £500	might pay in rent, rates, and taxes, £85—	a proportion of his income which is equal to about *one-sixth.*
A poor man with 24s. a week, or £62 8s. a year,	might pay in rent, rates, and taxes, 8s. a week, or £20 16s. a year—	a proportion of his income which is equal to *one-third.*

If the man with £2,000 a year paid one-third of his income in rent, rates, and taxes, he would pay £666 a year, while the man with £500 a year would pay £166, and they would both be better able to afford these sums than the poor man is able to afford his £20 16s. Allowing that each of them has a wife and four children to maintain, there would at least be enough left in both families to give sufficient nourishment to every member. Fewer servants might be kept, there might be less travelling, plainer clothes, and less saving, but enough to eat there would be. But the poor man, having no expenditure other than food which can be cut down, is obliged, in order to pay one-third of his income in rent, to cut down food.

The chief item in every poor budget is rent, and on the whole and roughly speaking it is safe to say that a family with three or more children is likely to be spending between 7s. and 8s. a week on rent alone. Why do they spend so much when, as we see, it must mean cutting down such a primary necessary as food ?

To find the answer to this question, an analysis was made of the conditions of thirty-one families with three or more children who happened to come within the scope of the investigation. The analysis took the form of a comparison of the death-rate in those families as related to the number of children in each, the household allowance of each, and the amount paid in rent by each. Household allowance was chosen rather than wage, as being necessarily in closer touch with household expenditure than is the actual wage, from which a varying amount of pocket-money for the man is generally taken.

Amount paid in rent was chosen rather than number of rooms, because low rent, though often meaning fewer rooms, may quite as likely mean basement rooms, or unusually small rooms, or rooms in a very old cottage below the level of an alley-way. One good upstairs room may cost as much as a couple of dark and damp basement rooms, and, though that one room may mean horrible overcrowding for a family of five or six persons, it may nevertheless be a wiser and healthier home than the two-roomed basement, where the overcrowding would nominally be less. As a matter of fact, owing to insufficient beds and bedding, the whole family would probably sleep in one of the two basement rooms, and therefore the air space at night would be no more adequate than in one room upstairs, while bronchitis and rheumatism would be added to the dangers of overcrowding.

The percentages given in the little table on p. 26 are calculated approximately to the nearest whole number below.

It is interesting to note that, while the death-rate increases from nothing in the case of families with only three children to 40 per cent. and over in the case of families with ten or eleven children, the intermediate percentages do not follow in numerical order. Families with five children have a worse death-rate than families with six, seven, or eight.

In the same way, if you compare death-rates according to household allowances, the death-rate of families with between 20s. and 22s. a week is actually higher than that of families with less than 20s.

When, however, the amount paid in rent is the basis of the arrangement, the death-rate rises

THIRTY-ONE FAMILIES WITH THREE OR MORE CHILDREN TAKEN WITHIN THE INVESTIGATION.

Total of 186 children; 46 dead; death-rate, 24·7.

Arranged according to Number in Family.

Number born in Each Family.	Number of Families.	Number Dead.	Approximate Death-rate.
			Per Cent.
3	2	0	0
4	9	6	16
5	3	4	26
6	5	6	20
7	4	6	21
8	5	10	25
10	2	8	40
11	1	6	54

Arranged according to Household Allowance.

Allowance.	Number of Families.	Number of Children born.	Number Dead.	Approximate Death-rate
				Per Cent.
Over 22/0 a week..	11	73	11	15
20/0 to 22/0 ..	9	59	19	32
Less than 20/0 ..	11	54	16	29

Arranged according to Rent.

Rent.	Number of Families.	Number of Children born.	Number Dead.	Approximate Death-rate
				Per Cent.
Over 6/6 ..	12	72	9	12
6/0 to 6/6 ..	7	39	7	17
Less than 6/0 ..	12	75	30	40

(See Appendix A, p. 42.)

from 12 per cent. to 40 per cent. as the rent gets less.

It is hardly necessary to point out that the death-rate is a rough-and-ready test, and not to be considered as a close indication. If it were practicable to use the general health of those alive as well as the death-rate, it would be far better. Also, of course, no one of the three arrangements is independent of the other two. Moreover, the numbers are few. The results of the analysis, however, though proving nothing, were considered interesting enough to encourage the making of the same analysis of thirty-nine cases of families with three or more children, taken from the records of the weighing-room at Moffat's Institute (see p. 28). The two lists were kept separate, as the cases at Moffat's Institute had been passed by no doctor, and hereditary disease may be considered to be more rampant among them. Added to this the wages are, on the whole, lower than the wages of families within the limits of the investigation.

It is curious that the death-rate in the second table for families paying under 6s. rent is much the same as it is in the first. The great difference between the two tables lies in the far larger death-rate in families paying over 6s. rent shown in the second table, where disease and insecurity and poverty were certainly greater factors.

It is not pretended that the two tables do more

Thirty-nine Families with Three or More Children taken from without the Investigation.

Total of 223 children; 70 dead; death-rate, 31·3.

Arranged according to Number in Family.

Number born in Each Family.	Number of Families.	Number Dead.	Approximate Death-rate.
			Per Cent.
3	7	2	9
4	7	4	14
5	6	15	50
6	7	11	26
7	4	8	28
8	2	2	12
9	4	21	58
11	2	7	31

Arranged according to Household Allowance.

Allowance.	Number of Families.	Number of Children born.	Number Dead.	Approximate Death-rate.
				Per Cent.
Over 22/0 a week ..	8	60	20	33
20/0 to 22/0 ..	20	111	34	30
Less than 20/0 ..	11	52	16	30

Arranged according to Rent.

Rent.	Number of Families.	Number of Children born.	Number Dead.	Approximate Death-rate.
				Per Cent.
Over 6/6	15	105	26	24
6/0 to 6/6 ..	14	71	26	36
Less than 6/0 ..	10	47	18	38

(See Appendix B, p. 44.)

than indicate that decent housing has as much influence on children's health as, given a certain minimum, the quality and quantity of their food. That is to say, it is as important for a young child to have light, air, warmth, and freedom from damp, as it is for it to have sufficient and proper food.

The kind of dwelling to be had for 7s. or 8s. a week varies in several ways. If it be light, dry, and free from bugs, if it be central in position, and if it contain three rooms, it will be eagerly sought for and hard to find. Such places exist in some blocks of workmen's dwellings, and applications for them are waiting long before a vacancy occurs, provided, of course, that they are in a convenient district. There are even sets of three very small rooms at a rental of 5s. 6d. in one or two large buildings. These are few in number, snapped up, and tend to go to the man with not too large a family and in a recognised and permanent position.

Perhaps the next best bargain after such rooms in blocks of workmen's dwellings is a portion of a small house. These small houses are let at rents varying from 10s. to 15s., according to size, condition, and position. They are let to a tenant who is responsible to the landlord for the whole rent, and who sublets such rooms as she can do without in order to get enough money for the rent-collector. She is often a woman with five or six children, who would not, on account of her

large family, be an acceptable subtenant. If
she is a good woman of business, it is sometimes
possible for her to let her rooms advantageously,
and stand in herself at a low rental—as rents go
in Lambeth. But there is always a serious risk
attached to the taking of a whole house—the risk
of not being able to sublet, or, if there are tenants,
of being unable to make them pay. Many a
woman who nominally stands at a rent of 6s. or
6s. 6d. for the rooms which she keeps for her own
use is actually paying 11s. to 15s. a week, or is
running into debt at the rate of 5s. to 10s. a
week because of default on the part of her lodgers.

The ordinary housing for 8s. a week consists
generally of three rooms out of a four-roomed
house where the responsible tenant pays 10s. or
11s. for the whole, and sublets one small room
for 2s. to 3s., or of three or four rooms out of a
five- or six-roomed house where the whole rent
might be 14s. or 15s., and a couple of rooms
may be sublet at 6s. or 7s. Some of the older
four-roomed houses are built on a terrible plan.
The passage from the front door runs along one
side of the house straight out at the back. Two
tiny rooms open off it, a front one and a back
one. Between these two rooms, at right angles
to the passage, ascends a steep flight of stairs.
Because of the narrowness of the house the stairs
have no landing at the top, but continue as stairs
until they meet the wall. Where the landing
should be, but is not, two doors leading into a

front bedroom and a back stand opposite one
another, and open directly on to the steps themselves. Coming out of a bedroom with a child
in their arms, obscuring their own light from the
door behind them, many a man and woman in
Lambeth has trodden on the edge of a step and
fallen down the stairs to the ground below. There
is no hand-rail, nothing but the smooth wall on
each side.

Of the four little rooms contained in such a
house, perhaps not one will measure more than
12 feet the longer way, and there may be a copper
wedged into the tiny kitchen. A family of eight
persons using three rooms in a house of this kind
might let off the lower front room to an aunt or
a mother at a rent of 2s. 6d. a week, live in the
kitchen, and sleep in the two upstairs rooms.
The advantage of such a way of living is its
privacy. The single lodger, even if not a relative,
is less disturbing than would be another family
sharing another house. When the lodger is a
relative, a further advantage is that a child is
often taken into its grandmother's or aunt's room
at night, and the terrible overcrowding is relieved
just to that extent.

In some districts four rooms may be had for
8s. a week—on the further side of Kennington
Park, for instance. Here the plan of the house
is more modern. The stairs face the front door,
have a hand-rail and any light which the passage
affords. The front room may be 12 feet square,

and the kitchen, cut into by the stairs, 10 feet square. There is a tiny scullery at the back, which is of enormous value, as the 10 feet square kitchen is the living-room of the family—sure to be a fairly large one or it would not take four rooms. Upstairs are three rooms. Two at the back will be very small, and the front one, extending the whole breadth of the house, perhaps 15 feet by 12 feet. A family of ten persons, now living in a house like this, lets off one of the small back bedrooms at a rental of 2s., and occupies the four remaining rooms at a cost of 8s. a week. The copper belongs to the woman renting the house, who makes what arrangements she pleases with her lodger in regard to its use.

There are four-roomed cottages in Lambeth where there is no passage at all. The front door opens into the front room. The room behind opens out of the front room. The stairs lead out of the room behind, and twist up so as to serve two communicating rooms above. Here the upstairs tenants are forced to pass through both the rooms of the lower tenants every time they enter or leave the house. The inconvenience and annoyance of this is intense. Both exasperated families live on the edge of bitter feud.

There are two-roomed cottages reached by alley-ways, where both tiny rooms are below the level of the pathetic garden at the door. Here one sanitary convenience serves for two cottages.

Here the death-rate would be high, but not so high as the death-rate in the dismal basements.

Where two families share a six-roomed house, the landlady of the two probably chooses the ground-floor, with command over the yard and washing arrangements. The upstairs people contract with her for the use of the copper and yard on one day of the week. The downstairs woman hates having the upstairs woman washing in her scullery, and the upstairs woman hates washing there. Differences which result in " not speaking " often begin over the copper. Three rooms upstairs and three rooms downstairs would be the rule in such a house, the downstairs woman being answerable to the landlord for 13s. a week, and the upstairs woman paying her 6s. Each woman scrubs the stairs in turn—another fruitful source of difficulty. Some of these houses are frankly arranged for two families, although the landlord only recognises one tenant. In such cases, though there is but one copper, there will be a stove in an upstairs room. In some houses the upstairs people have to manage with an open grate and a hob, and nearly all of them have to carry water upstairs and carry it down again when dirty.

On the whole, the healthiest accommodation is usually to be found in well-managed large blocks of workmen's dwellings. This may be as dear as three rooms for 9s., or it may be as cheap as three very small rooms for 5s. 6d. The great advantages are freedom from damp, freedom from bugs, light and air on the upper floors, water laid on, sometimes a yard where the children can play, safe from the traffic of the street. But there are disadvantages. The want of privacy, which is very great in the cheaper buildings, the tendency to take infection from other families, the noise on the stairs, the inability to keep a perambulator, are some of them. Then there is no such thing as keeping the landlord waiting. The rent must be paid or the tenant must quit. The management of most buildings exacts one or two weeks' rent in advance in order to be on the safe side. A tenant thus has one week up her sleeve, as it were, but gets notice directly she enters on that week. In some buildings the other people, kindly souls, will lend the rent to a steady family in misfortune. A carter's wife—one of the cases in the investigation—had her rent paid for ten weeks, while her husband was out of work and bringing in odd sums far below his usual wage, by the kindness of the neighbours, who saw her through. She was in good buildings, paying a low rent, and as she said, " If I'd a-got out of this I'd never a-got in agen." She paid off the money when her husband was in work again at the rate of 3s. 6d. a week.

The three-quarters of a small house or the half of a larger house are likely to be less healthy than " buildings," because houses are less well-built, often damp, often infested with bugs which defy the cleanest woman, have as a rule no water above the ground-floor, and may have fearful draughts and no proper fireplace. Their advantages are the superior privacy and possibly superior quiet, their accessibility from the street, and, above all, the elasticity with regard to rent. On the whole, the actual landlord is by no means the monster he is popularly represented to be. He will wait rather than change a good tenant. He will make no fuss if the back rent is paid ever so slowly. To many respectable folk, keeping the home together on perhaps 22s. a week, this is an inestimable boon. It is wonderful how, among these steady people, rent is made a first charge on income, though naturally, given enough pressure, rent must wait while such income as there is goes to buy food.

Rents of less than 6s. a week are generally danger-signals, unless the amount is for a single room. Two rooms for 5s. 6d. are likely to be basement rooms or very small ground-floor rooms, through one of which, perhaps, all the other people in the house have to pass. One of two such rooms visited for fifteen months measured 8 feet by 12 feet, had doors in three sides of it, and was the only means of exit at the back of the house.

Two sets of basement rooms at 5s 6d. visited during the investigation were extremely dark and damp. In both cases the amount of coal burned was unusually large, as was also the amount of gas. One of these basements was reached by stairs from within the house, the other from a deep area without. The former was warmer, but more airless, while the latter was impossible to warm in any way. The airlessness of basement dwellings is much enhanced by the police regulations, which insist on shut windows at night on account of the danger of burglary! Both the women in these two homes were languid and pale, and suffered from anæmia. The first had lost three children out of seven; the second, one out of four.

Four and six paid for two rooms meant two tiny rooms below the level of the alley-way outside—rooms which measured each about 12 feet square. A family of six persons lived in them. Four children were living, and five had died.

The question of vermin is a very pressing one in all the small houses. No woman, however clean, can cope with it. Before their confinements some women go to the trouble of having the room they are to lie in fumigated. In spite of such precautions, bugs have dropped on to the pillow of the sick woman before the visitor's eyes. One woman complained that they dropped into her ears at night. Another woman, when the visitor cheerily alluded to the lovely weather, answered in a voice of deepest gloom: " Lovely fer you, miss, but it brings out the bugs somethink 'orrible." The mothers accept the pest as part of their dreadful lives, but they do not grow reconciled to it. Repapering and fumigation are as far as any landlord goes in dealing with the difficulty, and it hardly needs saying that the effects of such treatment are temporary only. On suggesting distemper rather than a new paper in a stuffy little room, the visitor was met with the instant protest: " But it wouldn't keep the bugs out a minute." It would seem as though the burning down of such properties were the only cure.

The fault is not entirely that either of the sanitary authorities or of the immediate landlords. Nor is the blame to be given to the people living in these houses. In spite of being absurdly costly, they are too unhealthy for human habitation. Sanitation has improved vastly in the last dozen years, though there is still a great need for more qualified, authoritative women sanitary inspectors. But no inspection and no subsequnt tinkering can make a fundamentally unhealthy house a proper home for young children. The sanitary standard is still deplorably low. That is simply because it has to be low if some of these houses are to be considered habitable at all, and if others are to be inhabited by two, and often by three, families at the same time.

The landlords might use a different system with advantage to the great majority of their tenants. To insist on letting a whole house to tenants who are invariably unable to afford the rent of it is to contract out of half the landlord's risks, and to leave them on the shoulders of people far less able to bear them. A woman who can barely stagger under a rent of 6s., 7s., or 8s., may at any moment find herself confronted with a rent of 10s. 6d. or 15s., because, in her desperate desire to let at all, she is forced to accept an unsatisfactory tenant. Turned into a landlord in her own person, she is wonderfully long-suffering and patient, but at the cost of the food of her family. If ejectment has to be enforced, she, not the real landlord, has to enforce it. She goes through great stress rather than resort to it. Houses intended for the use of more than one family should, I consider, be definitely let off to more than one family. Each tenant should deal direct with the landlord.

The tenants might do more for themselves if they understood and could use their rights—if they expected to be more comfortable than they are. They put up with broken and defective grates which burn twice the coal for half the heat; they accept plagues of rats or of vermin as acts of God; they deplore a stopped-up drain without making an effective complaint, because they are afraid of being told to find new quarters if they make too much fuss. If they could or would take concerted action, they could right a great many of the smaller grievances. But, when all is said and done, these reforms could do very little as long as most of the present buildings exist at all, or as long as a family of eight persons can only afford two, or at most three, small rooms to live in. The rent is too dear; the houses are too old or too badly built, or both; the streets are too narrow; the rooms are too small; and there are far too many people to sleep in them.

The question is often asked why the people live where they do. Why do they not live in a district where rents are cheaper, and spend more on tram fares ? The reason is that these over-burdened women have no knowledge, no enter-prise, no time, and no cash, to enable them to visit distant suburbs along the tram routes, even if, in their opinion, the saving of money in rent would be sufficient to pay the extra outlay on tram fares. Moreover—strange as it may seem to those whose bi-weekly visit to Lambeth is like a bi-weekly plunge into Hades—the people to whom Lambeth is home want to stay in Lambeth. They do not expect to be any better off elsewhere, and meantime they are in surroundings they know, and among people who know and respect them. Probably they have relatives near by who would not see them come to grief without making great efforts to help them. Should the man go into hospital or into the workhouse infirmary, extraordinary kindness to the wife and children will be shown by the most stand-off neighbours, in order to keep the little household together until he is well again. A family who have lived for years in one street are recognised up and down the length of that street as people to be helped in time of trouble. These respectable but very poor people live over a morass of such intolerable poverty that they unite instinctively to save those known to them from falling into it. A family which moves two miles away is completely lost to view. They never write, and there is no time and no money for visiting. Neighbours forget them. It was not mere personal liking which united them; it was a kind of mutual respect in the face of trouble. Even relatives cease to be actively interested in their fate. A fish-fryer lost his job in Lambeth owing to the business being sold and the new owner bringing in his own fryer. The man had been getting 26s. a week, and owed nothing. His wife's brothers and parents, who lived near by, combined to feed three of the four children; a certain amount of coal was sent in; the rent was allowed to stand over by a sympathetic landlady to whom the woman had been kind in her confinement; and at last, after nine weeks, the man got work at Finsbury Park at 24s. a week. Nearly £3 was owing in rent, but otherwise there was no debt. The family stayed on in the same rooms, paying 3s. a week extra as back rent, and the man walked daily from south of Kennington Park to Finsbury Park and back. He started at five in the morning, arrived at eight, and worked till noon, when he had four hours off and a meal. He was allowed to lie down and sleep till 4 p.m. Then he worked again till 10 p.m., afterwards walking home, arriving there at about one in the morning. A year of this life knocked him up, and he left his place at Finsbury Park to find one in a fish-shop in Westminster at a still slightly lower wage. The back rent is long ago paid off, and the family, now with five children, is still in the same rooms, though in reduced circumstances. When questioned as to why he had remained in Kennington instead of moving after his work, the man pointed out that the back rent would seem almost impossible to pay off at a distance. Then there was no one who knew them at Finsbury, where, should misfortune overtake them again, instead of being helped through a period of unemployment, they would have nothing before them but the " house."

It is obvious that, in London at any rate, the wretched housing, which is at the same time more than they can afford, has as bad an influence on the health of the poor as any other of their miserable conditions. If poverty did not mean wretched housing, it would be shorn of half its dangers. The London poor are driven to pay one-third of their income for dark, damp rooms which are too small and too few in houses which are ill-built and overcrowded. And above the overcrowding of the house and of the room comes the overcrowding of the bed—equally the result of poverty, and equally dangerous to health. Even if the food which can be provided out of 22s. a week, after 7s. or 8s. has been taken for rent, were of first-rate quality and sufficient in quantity, the night spent in such beds in such rooms in such houses would devitalise the children. It would take away their appetites, and render them more liable to any infection at home or at school. Taken in conjunction with the food they do get, it is no wonder that the health of London school-children exercises the mind of the medical officials of the London County Council.

APPENDIX A

LIST OF THIRTY-ONE FAMILIES, WITHIN THE INVESTIGATION, FROM WHICH TABLE OF COMPARISON IS COMPILED.

	Allowance to Wife.	Children born.	Dead.	Rent.
Printer's warehouse-man	20/0	4	0	8/0
Printer's labourer..	28/0	8	0	8/0
Dustman	25/0	4	0	7/0
Policeman ..	27/0	8	1	8/6
Bus conductor ..	18/0	5	0	9/0
Coal carter ..	22/0	4	1	7/0
Plumber's mate ..	24/0	10	3	8/0
Horse-keeper ..	22/0	8	2	7/6
Printer's labourer	21/9	7	1	8/0
Railway - carriage washer	19/6	3	0	7/0
Packer of pottery	23/0	6	0	7/3
Carman's trouncer	24/0	5	1	8/0
Horse-keeper ..	23/0	3	0	6/6
Plumber's labourer	18/0	6	3	6/6
Potter's labourer..	20/0	4	0	6/0
Carter	19/0	4	1	6/0
Builder's handyman	22/6	7	1	6/6
Postal-van driver..	23/0	8	1	6/6

APPENDIX A—*Continued*

	Allowance to Wife.	Children born.	Dead.	Rent.
Labourer	22/6	7	1	6/0
Carter	15/0 to 20/0	6	1	5/0*
Pugilist	Very irregular; average below 20/0	8	6	5/0
Builder's labourer	Irregular; average below 20/0	6	1	3/0
Fish-fryer	23/0	7	3	5/6
Carter for vestry contractor	19/0	4	0	4/6*
Motor-car washer	Irregular; below 20/0	4	1	3/3
Butcher's assistant	Irregular; below 20/0	4	1	5/6
Scene-shifter ..	22/0	11	6	5/0
Carman	Below 20/0	4	2	4/6
Carter	20/0	10	5	4/6
Feather-cleaner's assistant	20/0	5	3	5/0
Borough Council street-sweeper	21/0	6	1	5/6

* These rooms are in buildings, upstairs and sanitary.

APPENDIX B

LIST OF THIRTY-NINE FAMILIES WITH THREE OR MORE CHILDREN, OUTSIDE THE INVESTIGATION, FROM WHICH TABLE OF COMPARISON IS COMPILED

	Allowance to Wife.	Children born.	Dead.	Rent.
Bricklayer's labourer	25/0	9	4	8/0
Music-seller's assistant in West-End shop	18/0	3	0	9/0
Carman	24/0	8	1	7/3
Postman	23/6	4	0	7/6
Baker's van-man ..	22/0	7	1	7/6
Stonemason ..	20/0	8	1	8/0
Carman	20/0	4	0	7/0
Sawmill labourer	20/0	5	1	6/0
Carman	22/0	4	1	6/6
House - decorator's labourer	Irregular; average less than 20/0	6	2	7/6
Labourer	Less than 20/0	3	1	4/0
Painter's labourer	Less than 20/0	3	0	6/6
Builder's labourer	Less than 20/0	6	0	8/0
Carman	18/0	4	1	6/0
Waterside labourer	Less than 20/0	5	3	4/0

APPENDIX B—*Continued*

	Allowance to Wife.	Children born.	Dead.	Rent.
Brass-foundry core-maker	24/0	3	1	6/6
Labourer	22/0	4	1	6/0
Shop-assistant ..	20/0	4	1	6/0
Carman	20/0	6	4	6/6
Painter's labourer..	20/0	7	3	7/6
Carman	20/0	3	0	4/6
Carman	18/6	7	3	4/0
Stone-grinder ..	20/0	3	0	5/6
Goods porter ..	25/0	5	2	7/0
Cleaner for L.G.B.	22/0	3	0	6/6
Carman	20/0	6	1	6/6
Stoker	24/0	11	3	8/0
Carman	22/0	9	4	7/6
Potter's labourer ..	Less than 20/0	5	4	5/0
Labourer	Less than 20/0	4	0	4/0
Painter's labourer..	21/0	5	2	6/0
Gas-worker ..	20/0	6	0	6/0
Blacksmith's labourer	18/0	6	2	4/9
Carman	24/0	9	5	6/0
Labourer in timber-yard	20/0	5	3	5/6
Carman for brewery	20/0	6	2	5/0
Tin-plate worker ..	24/0	11	4	8/0
Van-washer ..	20/0	9	8	6/0
Carman	20/0	7	1	8/0

CHAPTER IV

FURNITURE—SLEEPING ACCOMMODATION—EQUIP-MENT FOR COOKING AND BATHING

It is difficult to say whether more furniture or less furniture would be the better plan in a home consisting of three rooms. Supposing the family to consist of eight persons, most people would be inclined to prescribe four beds. As a matter of fact, there will probably be two. In a double bed in one room will sleep father, mother, baby, and ex-baby, while in another bed in another room will sleep the four elder children. Sometimes the lodger granny will take a child into her bed, or the lodger uncle will take a boy into his; but the four in a bed arrangement is common enough to need attention. It must be remembered again that these people are respectable, hard-working, sober, and serious. They keep their jobs, and they stay on in the same rooms. They are not slum people. They pay their rent with wonderful regularity, and are trusted by the landlord when for any reason they are obliged to hold it back. But, all the same, they have to sleep four in a bed, and suffer the consequences. It is not an elastic arrangement; in case of illness it goes on just the same. When a child has a sore throat or a rash it sleeps with the others as usual. By the time a medical authority has pronounced the illness to be diphtheria or scarlet fever, and the child is taken away, perhaps another child is infected. Measles and whooping-cough just go round the bed as a matter of course. When a new baby is born, the mother does not get her bed to herself. There is nowhere for the others to go, so they sleep in their accustomed places. This is not a fact which obtrudes itself on the notice of a visitor as a rule. She arrives to find the mother and child alone in the bed, with the exception, perhaps, of a two-year-old having its daily nap at the foot. But in a case where there was but one room, and where the man was a night-worker, the visitor of the sick woman found him asleep beside her. This discovery led to questions being put to the other women, who explained at once that of course their husbands and children sleep with them at night. Where else is there for the unfortunate people to sleep? Moreover, the husband is probably needed to act as monthly nurse at night for the first week. It is an arrangement which does not allow of real rest for any of them, but it has to be put up with.

The rooms are small, and herein lies the open-window difficulty far more than in the ignorance of the women. Poor people dread cold. Their one idea in clothing their children is to keep them warm. To this end they put on petticoat over ragged petticoat till the children are fettered by the number of garments. It is not the best method, but it is the best method they know of. The best, of course, would be so to feed the children that their bodies would generate enough heat to keep them warm from within without unnecessary clothing. A second-best method might be to clothe the badly-nourished bodies warmly and lightly from without. The best they can do is to load the children with any kind of clothing they can procure, be it light and warm or cold and heavy. The best is too expensive; the second-best is too expensive; and so they have recourse to the third. It is all they can do with the means at their disposal. So with sleeping and fresh air. The best arrangement is a large room, a bed to oneself, plenty of bedclothes, and an open window. The second-best is a small room, a bed for every two persons, plenty of bedclothes, and an open window. The only arrangement actually possible is a tiny room, one bed for four people, one blanket or two very thin ones, with the bed close under the window. In wet or very cold weather the four people in the bed sleep with the window shut. What else can they do ? Here are some cases each visited for over a year during the investigation:

1. Man, wife, and three children; one room, 12 feet by 10 feet; one bed, one banana-crate cot. Man a night-worker. Wages varying from 16s. to 20s. Bed, in which woman and two children

slept all night, and man most of the day, with its head half across the window; cot right under the window.

2. Man, wife, and four children; one room, 12 feet by 14 feet; one bed, one cot, one banana-crate cot. Wage from 19s. to 22s. The bed and small cot stood alongside the window; the other cot stood across it.

3. Man, wife, and six children; four rooms; two beds, one sofa, one banana-crate cot. Wage 22s. One double bed for four people in very small room, crossing the window; cot in corner by bed. One single bed for two people (girls aged thirteen and ten years) in smaller room, 8 feet by 10 feet, with head under the window. One sofa for boy aged eleven years in front downstairs room, where police will not allow window to be open at night. The kitchen, which is at the back, has the copper in it, and is too small for a bed, or even a sofa to stand anywhere.

4. Man, wife, and five children; two rooms; one bed, one sofa, one perambulator. Wage 22s. One bed for four persons across window in tiny room; perambulator for baby by bed; one sofa for two boys in kitchen, also tiny.

5. Man, wife, and four children; two basement rooms; one bed, one baby's cot, one sofa. One bed for four, with baby's cot by it, in one room; sofa for child of nine in the other. In front room the police will not allow the window open at night.

6. Man, wife, and five children; three small

rooms upstairs; two beds, one cot; one double bed for three persons, with head to window, cot beside it, in one room; one wide single bed for three persons across window in other room.

7. Man, wife, and five children; two rooms upstairs; one wide single bed, one narrow single bed, one cot. Wife sleeps with two children in wide single bed, baby in cot by her side. Two children under window in tiny back room in narrow single bed. The man works at night, and gets home about four in the morning. He sits up n a chair till six o'clock, when his wife gets up and makes up the children's bed in the back room for him.

There are plenty more of such cases. Those above have been taken at random from an alphabetical list. In one a woman and five children sleep in one room, but, as it is large enough to have two windows, they can keep one open, and are better off than many parties of four in smaller rooms, where the bed perforce comes under the only window.

It may be noticed that in some of the cases given, as in some which I have no space to give, a third or fourth room, which is generally the living-room, has no one sleeping in it at night. The women, when asked why they do not relieve the pressure in the family bedroom by putting a child or two in the kitchen, explain that they have no more beds and no more bedclothes. Each fresh bed needs blankets and mattress. They look round the tiny room, and ask, " Where'd I put it if I 'ad it ?"   Besides, to put a couple of children to bed in the one living-room makes it both a bad bedroom and a bad sitting-room, even if the initial difficulty of bed and bedding could be overcome.

It will be noticed, too, that in the list given a cot of some sort was always provided for the little baby.   Unfortunately, this is not a universal rule.   It appears here because the investigation insisted on the new baby having a cot to itself. Otherwise it would have taken its chance in the family bed.   In winter the mothers find it very difficult to believe that a new-born baby can be warm enough in a cot of its own.   And when one looks at the cotton cot blankets, about 30 inches long, which are all their wildest dreams aspire to, one understands their disbelief.   The cost of a cot at its cheapest runs as follows: Banana-crate with sacking bottom, 1s.; bag filled with chaff for mattress, 2d.; blankets, 1s. 6d. bought whole-sale and sold at cost price.   This mounts up to 2s. 8d., and, for a woman who has to buy blankets at an ordinary shop, a quality good enough for the purpose would cost her more.   She would have to spend something like 3s. 6d. over the child's cot—a sum which is beyond the reach of most women with a 20s. budget.   As a rule it would be safe to say that the new baby does take its share of the risks of the family bed, legislation to the contrary notwithstanding.

The rest of the furniture is both as insufficient and crowded as is the sleeping accommodation. There are not enough chairs, though too many for the room. There is not enough table space, though too much for the room. There is no wardrobe accommodation other than the hook behind the door, and possibly a chest of drawers, which may partly act as a larder, and has in the visitor's experience been used as a place in which to put a dead child.

To take an actual case of a one-room tenement. There are four children, all living. The man is a dusky, friendly soul who usually addresses an elderly visitor as " mate." On first making his acquaintance, the visitor was so much struck by the brilliance of his teeth shining from his grimy face, that she ventured to express her admiration. " Yes, mate, an' I tell yer why: 'cause I cleans 'em," he answered delightedly, and after a short pause added, " once a week." On one occasion the visitor, noticing that a slight pressure was needed on a certain part of the baby's person, looked for a penny in her purse, found none, but was supplied by the interested father. The penny was quickly stitched into a bandage, and tied firmly over the required place. The next week saw the family in dire need of a penny to put in the gas-meter in order to save the dinner from being uncooked. At the moment of crisis a flash of genius inspired the father; the baby was undressed, the penny disinterred, and the dinner saved. The visitor, arriving in the middle of the scene, could but accept the position, sacrifice a leaden weight which kept the tail of her coat hanging as it should, and rebandage the baby.

The single room inhabited by this family is large—15 feet by 13 feet—and has two windows. Under the window facing the door is the large bed, in which sleep mother, father, and two children. A perambulator by the bedside accommodates the baby, and in the further corner is a small cot for the remaining child. The second window can be, and is, left partly open at night. At the foot of the bed which crosses the window is a small square table. Three wooden chairs and a chest of drawers complete the furniture, with the exception of a treadle machine purchased by the mother before her marriage on the time-payment system. The small fireplace has no oven, and open shelves go up each side of it. There are two saucepans, both burnt. There is no larder. On the floor lies a loose piece of linoleum, and over the fireplace is an overmantel with brackets and a cracked looking-glass. On the brackets are shells and ornaments. Tiny home-made window-boxes with plants in them decorate each window. The whole aspect of the room is cheerful. It is not stuffy, because the second window really is always open. The overmantel was saved for penny by penny before marriage, and is much valued. It gives the room an air, as its mistress proudly says.

Another family with eight children, all living, rent four rooms—two downstairs and two up. Downstairs is a sitting-room 10 feet by 12 feet. In it are a sofa, a table, four chairs, and the perambulator. A kitchen 10 feet by 10 feet contains a tiny table and six chairs. The cupboard beside the stove has mice in it. A gas-stove stands in the washhouse beside the copper. By it there is room for a cupboard for food, but it is a very hot cupboard in the summer. One bedroom with two windows, upstairs, has a large bed away from the window, in which sleep mother and three children. The baby sleeps in a cot beside the bed, and in a small cot under one window sleeps a fifth child. One chair and a table complete the furniture. In another bedroom, 10 feet by 8 feet, sleep two children in a single bed by night, and the father, who is a night-worker, and any child taking its morning rest, by day. The remaining child sleeps on the sofa downstairs, where the window has to be shut at night.

Another family with six children rent three rooms. The kitchen has the copper in it, and measures 12 feet by 10 feet. A table of 4 feet by 2 feet under the window, three chairs, a mantel-shelf, and a cupboard high up on the wall, complete the furniture. Food can be kept in a perforated box next the dust-hole by the back door. The room has a tiny recess under the stairs beside the stove, where stands the perambulator in the daytime, though it goes upstairs to form the baby's bed at night.   In one bedroom, 12 feet by 10 feet, is a big bed near the window, in which sleep father, mother, and one child, with the baby by the bedside.   In another smaller room sleep four children under the window, in one bed. No other furniture.

It will be noticed that in none of the bedrooms are any washing arrangements.   The daily ablutions, as a rule, are confined to face and hands when each person comes downstairs, with the exception of the little baby, who generally has some sort of wash over every day.   Once a week, however, most of the children get a bath.   In the family of eight children mentioned above, the baby has a daily bath in the washing-up basin. On Friday evenings two boys and a girl under five years of age are bathed, all in the same water, in a washing-tub before the kitchen fire.   On Saturday nights two boys under eleven bathe in one water, which is then changed, and two girls of nine and twelve take their turn, the mother also washing their hair. The mother manages to bathe herself once a fortnight in the daytime when the five elder children are at school, and the father goes to public baths when he can find time and afford twopence.

A woman with six children under thirteen gives them all a bath with two waters between them on Saturday morning in the washing-tub. She generally has a bath herself on Sunday evening when her husband is out.   All the water has to be carried upstairs, heated in her kettle, and carried down again when dirty. Her husband bathes, when he can afford twopence, at the public baths.

In another family, where there are four children in one room and only a very small washtub, the children get a bath on Saturday or Sunday. The mother manages to get hers when the two elder children are at school. The father, who can never afford a twopenny bath, gets a " wash-down " sometimes after the children have gone to sleep at night. " A bath it ain't, not fer grown-up people," explained his wife; " it's just a bit at a time like." Some families use the copper when it is built in the kitchen or in a well-built scullery. But it is more trouble to empty, and often belongs to the other people's part of the house. All of these bathing arrangements imply a great deal of hard work for the mother of the family. Where the rooms are upstairs and water is not laid on, which is the case in a great many first-floor tene-ments, the work is excessive.

The equipment for cooking is as unsatisfactory as are the arrangements for sleeping or bathing. One kettle, one frying-pan, and two saucepans, both burnt, are often the complete outfit. The woman with 22s. a week upon which to rear a family may not be a professed cook and may not understand food values—she would probably be a still more discouraged woman than she is if she were and if she did—but she knows the weak

points of her old saucepans, and the number of
pennies she can afford to spend on coal and gas,
and the amount of time she can allow herself in
which to do her cooking. She is forced to give
more weight to the consideration of possible time
and possible money than to the considerations of
excellence of cooking or extra food value. Also
she must cook for her husband food which he likes
rather than food which she may consider of
greater scientific value, which he may dislike.

The visitors in this investigation hoped to
carry with them a gospel of porridge to the hard-
worked mothers of families in Lambeth. The
women of Lambeth listened patiently, according
to their way, agreed to all that was said, and did
not begin to feed their families on porridge.
Being there to watch and note rather than to
teach and preach, the visitors waited to hear,
when and how they could, what the objection
was. It was not one reason, but many. Porridge
needs long cooking; if on the gas, that means
expense; if on an open fire, constant stirring and
watching just when the mother is most busy
getting the children up. Moreover, the fire is
often not lit before breakfast. It was pointed
out that porridge is a food which will keep when
made. It could be cooked when the children are
at school, and merely warmed up in the morning.
The women agreed again, but still no porridge.
It seemed, after further patient waiting on the
part of the visitors, that the husbands and chil-

dren could not abide porridge—to use the expressive language of the district, " they 'eaved at it."

Why ? Well cooked the day before, and eaten with milk and sugar, all children liked porridge. But the mothers held up their hands. Milk ! Who could give milk—or sugar either, for that matter ? Of course, if you could give them milk and sugar, no wonder ! They might eat it then, even if it was a bit burnt. Porridge was an awful thing to burn in old pots if you left it a minute; and if you set the pot flat on its bottom instead of holding it all to one side to keep the burnt place away from the flame, it would " ketch " at once. An' then, if you'd happened to cook fish or " stoo " in the pot for dinner, there was a kind of taste come out in the porridge. It was more than they could bear to see children who was 'ungry, mind you, pushin' their food away or 'eavin' at it. So it usually ended in a slice of " bread and marge " all round, and a drink of tea, which was the breakfast they were accustomed to. One woman wound up a long and patient explanation of why she did not give her husband porridge with: " An', besides, my young man 'e say, Ef you gives me that stinkin' mess, I'll throw it at yer." Those were the reasons. It is true that to make porridge a good pot which is not burnt, and which is not used for " fish or stoo," is needed. It is also true that to eat porridge with the best results milk is needed. If neither of these necessaries can be obtained, porridge is apt to be burnt or half cooked, and is in either case very unpalatable. Children do not thrive on food they loathe, and men who are starting for a hard day's work refuse even to consider the question. What is the mother to do ? Of course, she gives them food they do like and can eat—bread and margarine or bread and jam, with a drop of hot weak tea. The women are very fond of Quaker oats when they can afford the luxury, and if milk is provided to drink with it. They can cook a little portion in a tin enamelled cup, and so escape the family saucepan.

Another difficulty which dogs the path of the Lambeth housekeeper is, either that there is no oven or only a gas oven which requires a good deal of gas, or that the stove oven needs much fuel to heat it. Once a week, for the Sunday dinner, the plunge is taken. Homes where there is no oven send out to the bakehouse on that occasion. The rest of the week is managed on cold food, or the hard-worked saucepan and frying-pan are brought into play. The certainty of an economical stove or fireplace is out of the reach of the poor. They are often obliged to use old-fashioned and broken ranges and grates which devour coal with as little benefit to the user as possible. They are driven to cook by gas, which ought to be an excellent way of cooking, but under the penny-in-the-slot system it is a way which tends to underdone food.

Table appointments are never sufficient. The

children hardly sit down to any meal but dinner, and even then they sometimes stand round the table for lack of chairs. Some women have a piece of oilcloth on the table; some spread a newspaper. So many plates are put round, each containing a dinner. The eating takes no time at all. A drink of water out of a tea-cup which is filled for each child in turn finishes the repast.

Equipment for cleaning is one of the elastic items in a budget. A Lambeth mother would like to spend 5d. on soap, 1d. on soda, 1d. on blue and starch. She is obliged in many cases to compress the expenditure to 3d. or 5d. all told She sometimes has to make 2d. do. There is the remains of a broom sometimes. Generally there is only a bucket and a cloth, which latter, probably, is the quite hopelessly worn-out shirt or pinafore of a member of the family. One woman heard of soda which could be bought in The Walk for less than the traditional 7 pounds for 3d., and, in her great economy, supplied her house with this inferior kind. She scrubbed and washed and cleaned with it till her poor arms lost all their skin, and she was taken into the workhouse infirmary with dangerous blood-poisoning. There she stayed for many weeks, while sisters and sisters-in-law took care of her children at a slight charge for mere food, and the husband, who was earning steady wages, looked after himself. He said it was more expensive without her than with her, and never rested till he got her home again.

The cleaning of the house is mostly done in the afternoons, when dinner is disposed of. Scrubbing, grate-cleaning, bed-making, are attended to after the return to school and to work of the children and husband. The baby and ex-baby are persuaded to sleep then, if possible, while the mother, with due regard to economy of soap, cleans out her little world. She has hardly finished before the children are back for tea, and after tea the washing up.

Two pennyworth of soap may have to wash the clothes, scrub the floors, and wash the people of a family, for a week. It is difficult to realise the soap famine in such a household. Soda, being cheap, is made to do a great deal. It sometimes appears in the children's weekly bath; it often washes their hair. A woman who had been using her one piece of soap to scrub the floor next brought it into play when she bathed the baby, with the unfortunate result of a long scratch on the baby from a cinder in the soap. She sighed when the visitor noticed the scratch, and said: " I sometimes think I'd like a little oven best, but now it do seem as if I'd rather 'ave two bits of soap." The visitor helpfully suggested cutting the one piece in two, but the mother shook her experienced head, and said: " It wouldn't last not 'arf as long."

Clothing is, frankly, a mystery. In the budgets of some women 6d. a week is set down opposite the item " clothing club " or " calico club." This seems meant to provide for underclothing—chiefly flannelette. One shilling is down, perhaps, against " boot club." Other provision in the most thrifty family there seems to be none. A patient visitor may extract information, perhaps, that the father gets overtime pay at Christmas, and applies some of it to the children's clothes, or that he is in a paying-out club which produces anything from 13s. to 26s., or thereabouts, at the end of the year. But in the great number of cases there is no extra money at Christmas, or at any other time, to depend upon. In the poorer budgets items for clothes appear at extraordinarily distant intervals, when, it is to be supposed, they can no longer be done without. " Boots mended " in the weekly budget means less food for that week, while any clothes which are bought seem to be not only second-hand, but in many instances fourth- or fifth-hand. In the course of fifteen months' visiting, one family on 23s. a week spent £3 5s. 5½d. on clothes for the mother and six children. Half the sum was spent on boots, so that the clothes other than boots of seven people cost 32s. 9d. in fifteen months—an average of 4s. 8d. a head. Another family spent 9d. a week on boots and 9d. a week on clothes in general. There were four children. Some families, again, only buy clothes when summer comes and less is needed for fuel. The clubs to which extra careful women, or women with more money for house-keeping, subscribe, are generally run by a small local tradesman. Whether they work for the benefit of their clients, or whether, as seems far more likely, they are run entirely in the interests of the proprietors, has not been a subject of research for the investigation. They fill a want. That is evident. Women bringing up a family on 20s. or even more a week need to have a definite expenditure in order to know where they are. They like to buy the same things week after week, because then they can calculate to a nicety how the money will last. They like to do their saving in the same way. So much a week regularly paid has a great attraction for them. If the club will, in addition to small regular payments, send someone to call for the amount, the transaction leaves nothing to be desired. A woman who can see her way towards the money by any possibility agrees at once. Payment by instalment fascinates the poor for the same reason. It is a regular amount which they can understand and grasp, and the awful risk, if misfortune occurs, of losing the precious article, together with such payments as have already been made, does not inflame their imaginations. If people living on £1 a week had lively imaginations, their lives, and perhaps the face of England, would be different.

Boots form by far the larger part of clothing expenses in a family of poor children. Most fathers in Lambeth can sole a little boot with some sort of skill. One man, a printer's handyman, spends some time every day over the boots of his children. He is a steady, intelligent man, and he says it takes him all his spare time. As soon as he has gone round the family the first pair is ready again. The women seldom get new clothes; boots they often are entirely without. The men go to work and must be supplied, the children must be decent at school, but the mother has no need to appear in the light of day. If very badly equipped, she can shop in the evening in The Walk, and no one will notice under her jacket and rather long skirt what she is wearing on her feet. Most of them have a hat, a jacket, and a " best " skirt, to wear in the street. In the house a blouse and a patched skirt under a sacking apron is the universal wear. Some of the women miraculously manage to look clean and tidy; some do not. The astonishing difference made by a new pink blouse, becomingly-done hair, and a well-made skirt, on one drab-looking woman who seemed to be about forty was too startling to forget. She suddenly looked thirty (her age was twenty-six), and she had a complexion and quite pretty hair—features never noticed before. These women who look to be in the dull middle of middle age are young; it comes as a shock when the mind grasps it.

In connection with clothing comes the vexed question of flannelette. To a mother, they all use it. It is warm, soft, and cheap. The skirts for two children's petticoats can be bought for 4d.— the bodies, too, if the children are tiny and skill is used. What else can the women buy that will serve its purpose as well ? It is inflammable—

the mothers know that, but they hope to escape accident—and it is cheap enough to buy. Better, they think, a garment of flannelette than no garment at all ! They would use material which is not inflammable if there were any they could afford which is as warm and soft and unshrinkable as flannelette. The shops to which their calico clubs belong stock flannelettes of all the most cheap and useful and inflammable kinds. Flannel, merino, cashmere, woollen material of any kind, are dear in comparison. Enough unshrinkable stuff to make a child a new warm, soft dress can be bought for 6d. A woman with 6d. to spend will buy that stuff rather than let her child go without the dress. It is what we should all do in her place. A child must be dressed. Give any London magistrate 6d. a week on which to dress four children; give him a great deal of cooking, scrubbing, and housework, to do; put a flannelette shop round the corner: in exactly four weeks each of those children would be clothed in flannelette.

The difficulty of keeping windows open at night; the impossibility—with the best will in the world —of bathing children more than once a week; the hasty and inadequate cooking in worn-out and cheap utensils; the clumsy, hampering, and ill-arranged clothing—all these things, combined with the housing conditions described in the previous chapter, show how difficult is the path of the woman entrusted, on a few shillings a week, with the health and lives of a number of future citizens.

CHAPTER V

THRIFT

It is just that a short chapter should be devoted to the thrift of such a class of wage-earners and their wives as are described here. It is a common idea that there is no thrift among them. It would be better for their childern if this were true. As a matter of fact, sums varying from 6d. a week to 1s. 6d., 1s. 8d., or even 2s., go out from incomes which are so small that these sums represent, perhaps, from 2½ to 10 per cent. of the whole household allowance. The object of this thrift is, unfortunately, not of the slightest benefit to the children of the families concerned. The money is spent or saved or invested, whichever is the proper term, on burial insurance. No living child is better fed or better clothed because its parents, decent folk, scrape up a penny a week to pay the insurance collector on its account. Rather is it less well fed and less well clothed to the extent of 1d. a week—an appreciable amount when it is, perhaps, one of eight persons living on £1 a week.

One of the criticisms levelled at these respectable, hard-working, independent people is that they do like to squander money on funerals. It is a view held by everyone who does not know the real circumstances. It is also held by many who do know them, but who confuse the fact that poor people show a great interest in one another's funerals with the erroneous idea that they could bury their dead for half the amount if they liked. Sometimes, in the case of adult men, this may be so. When alive, the man, perhaps, was a member of a society for burial benefit, and at his death the club or society bury him with much pomp and ceremony. In the case of the young children of people living on from 18s. to 30s. a week, the parents do not squander money on funerals which might be undertaken for half the price.

A working man and his wife who have a family are confronted with the problem of burial at once. They are likely to lose one or more of their children. The poorer they are, the more likely are they to lose them. Shall they run the risk of burial by the parish, or shall they take Time by the forelock and insure each child as it is born, at the rate of a penny a week ? If they decide not to insure, and they lose a child, the question resolves itself into one of borrowing the sum necessary to pay the funeral expenses, or of undergoing the disgrace of a pauper funeral. The pauper funeral carries with it the pauperization of the father of the child—a humiliation which adds disgrace to the natural grief of the parents. More than that, they declare that the pauper funeral is wanting in dignity and in respect to their dead. One woman expressed the feeling of many more when she said she would as soon have the dust-cart call for the body of her child as that " there Black Mariar." This may be sheer prejudice on the part of poor parents, but it is a prejudice which richer parents—even the most educated and highly born of them—if confronted with the same problem when burying their own children, would fully share. Refusing, then, if uninsured, to accept the pauper burial, with its consequent political and social degradation of a perfectly respectable family, the parents try to borrow the money needed. Up and down the street sums are collected in pence and sixpences, until the price of a child's funeral on the cheapest scale is secured. Funerals are not run on credit; but the neighbours, who may be absolute strangers, will contribute rather than suffer the degradation to pauperism of one of themselves. For months afterwards the mother and remaining children will eat less in order to pay back the money borrowed. The father of the family cannot eat less. He is already eating as little as will enable him to earn the family wage. To starve him would be bad economy. He must fare as usual. The rest of the family can eat less without bothering anybody—and do.

What is the sum necessary to stand between a working man and pauperdom should he suffer

the loss of a child ?   Inquiry among undertakers
in Lambeth and Kennington resulted in the discovery that a very young baby could be buried
by one undertaker for 18s., and by a dozen others
for 20s.   To this must be added the fee of 10s.
to the cemetery paid by the undertaker, which
brought his charges up to 28s. or 30s.   No firm
could be discovered who would do it for less.
When a child's body is too long to go under the
box-seat of the driver, the price of the funeral goes
up.   A sort of age scale is roughly in action,
which makes a funeral of a child of three more
expensive than that of a child of six months
Thirty shillings, then, is the lowest sum to be
faced by the grieving parents.   But how is a man
whose whole weekly income may be but two-
thirds of that amount to produce at sight 30s.
or more ?   Of course he cannot.   Sheer dread of
the horrible problem drives his wife to pay out
10d., 11d., or 1s., a week year after year—money
which, as far as the welfare of the children themselves go, might as well be thrown into the sea.

A penny a week paid from birth just barely
pays the funeral expenses as the child grows older.
It does not completely pay them in early infancy.
Thirteen weekly pennies must be paid before any
benefit is due, and the first sum due is not sufficient; but it is a help.   As each child must be
insured separately, the money paid for the child
who does not die is no relief when a death occurs.
Insurance, whether State or other insurance, is

always a gamble, and people on £1 a week cannot afford a gamble. A peculiar hardship attaches to burial insurance. A man may have paid regularly for years, may fall out of work through illness or other misfortune, and may lose all benefit. When out of work his children are more likely to die, and he may have to suffer the disgrace of a pauper funeral after five years or more of regular payment for burial insurance.

Great numbers of premature confinements occur among women who live the lives these wives and mothers do. A premature confinement, if the child breathes, means an uninsured funeral. True, an undertaker will sometimes provide a coffin which he slips into another funeral, evade the cemetery fee, and only charge 10s.; but even 10s. is a terrible sum to produce at the moment. Great is the anxiety on the part of the mother to be able to prove that her child was stillborn.

The three-year-old daughter of a carter out of work died of tuberculosis. The father, whose policies had lapsed, borrowed the sum of £2 5s. necessary to bury the child. The mother was four months paying the debt off by reducing the food of herself and of the five other children. The funeral cortège consisted of one vehicle, in which the little coffin went under the driver's seat. The parents and a neighbour sat in the back part of the vehicle. They saw the child buried in a common grave with twelve other coffins of all sizes. " We 'ad to keep a sharp eye out for Edie," they said; " she were so little she were almost 'id."

The following is an account kept of the funeral of a child of six months who died of infantile cholera in the deadly month of August, 1911. The parents had insured her for 2d. a week, being unusually careful people.   The sum received was £2.

	£	s.	d.
Funeral	1	12	0
Death certificate	0	1	3
Gravediggers	0	2	0
Hearse attendants	0	2	0
Woman to lay her out ..	0	2	0
Insurance agent	0	1	0
Flowers	0	0	6
Black tie for father	0	1	0
	2	1	9

The child was buried in a common grave with three others.   There is no display and no extravagance in this list.   The tips to the gravediggers, hearse attendants, and insurance agent, were all urgently applied for, though not in every case by the person who received the money.   The cost of the child's illness had amounted to 10s., chiefly spent on special food.   The survivors lived on reduced rations for two weeks in order to get square again.   The father's wage was 24s., every penny of which he always handed over to his wife.

The usual amount paid for burial insurance is 1d. a week for each child, 2d. for the mother, and 3d. for the father, making 11d. a week for a family with six children, though some over-cautious women make the sum more.

Another form of thrift is some sort of paying-out club. Usually payments of this kind come out of the father's pocket-money, but a few instances where the women made them came within the experience of the investigators. One club was named a " didly club." Its method seemed to consist in each member paying a certain woman $\frac{1}{4}$d. the first week, $\frac{1}{2}$d. the next week, $\frac{3}{4}$d. the next week, and so on, always adding $\frac{1}{4}$d. to the previous payment. The money was to be divided at Christmas. It was a mere way of saving, as no interest of any kind was to be paid. Needless to relate, about October the woman to whom the money had been paid disappeared. Stocking clubs, crockery clubs, and Christmas dinner clubs, make short appearances in the budgets. They usually entail a weekly payment of 3d. or 4d., and when the object — the children's winter stockings, the new plates, or the Christmas dinner—has been attained, the payments cease.

One form of money transaction which is hardly regarded as justifiable when poor people resort to it, but which at the same time is the ordinary, laudable, business custom of rich men —namely, borrowing—is carried on by the poor under very distressing conditions. When no friend or friends can be found to help at a crisis, many a woman has been driven—perhaps to pay the rent —to go to what she calls a lender. A few shillings are borrowed—perhaps five or six. The terms are a penny a week on every shilling borrowed, with, it may be, a kind of tip of half a crown at the end when all the principle and interest has been paid off. A woman borrowing 6s. pays 6d. a week in sheer interest—that is, £1 6s. a year—without reducing her debt a penny. She is paying 433 per cent. on her loan. She does not know the law, and she could not afford to invoke its aid if she did know it. She goes on being bled because it is the local accepted rate of a " lender." Only one of the women whose budgets appear in these pages has had recourse to this kind of borrowing, but the custom is well known by them all.

Such is the passion for weekly regular payments among these women that, had the Post Office initiated regular collection of pennies instead of the industrial insurance companies doing so, either the Post Office would now be in possession of the enormous accumulated capital of these companies, or the people on 20s. a week would have been much better off. The great bulk of the pennies so urgently needed for other purposes, and paid for burial insurance, is never returned in any form whatsoever to the people who pay them. The small proportion which does come to them is swallowed up in a burial, and no one but the undertaker is the better for it. As a form of thrift which shall help the future, or be a standby if misfortune should befall, burial insurance is a calamitous blunder. Yet the respectable poor man is forced to resort to it unless he is to run the risk of being made a pauper by any bereavement which may happen to him. It is a terrible object lesson in how not to manage. If the sum of £11,000,000 a year stated to be paid in weekly pennies by the poor to the industrial burial insurance companies were to be spent on better house room and better food—if, in fact, the one great universal thrift of the poor were not for death, but were for life—we should have a stronger nation. The only real solution of this horrible problem would seem to be the making of decent burial a free and honourable public service.

CHAPTER VI

BUDGETS

PERHAPS it will be as well here to reiterate the statement that these chapters are descriptive of the lives and conditions of families where the wage of the father is continuous, where he is a sober, steady man in full work, earning from 18s. to 30s. a week, and allowing a regular definite sum to his wife for all expenses other than his own clothes, fares, and pocket-money. Experience shows how fatally easy it is for people to label all poverty as the result of drink, extravagance, or laziness. It is done every day in the year by writers and speakers and preachers, as well as by hundreds of well-meaning folk with uneasy consciences. They see, or more often hear of, people whose economy is different from their own. Without trying to find out whether their own ideas of economy are practicable for the people in question, they dismiss their poverty as " the result of extravagance " or drink. Then they turn away with relief at the easy explanation. Or they see or hear of something which seems to them bad management. It may be, not good management, but the only management under the circumstances. But, as the circumstances are unknown, the description serves, and middle-class minds, only too anxious to be set at rest, are set at rest. Drink is an accusation fatally easy to throw about. By suggesting it you account for every difficulty, every sorrow. A man who suffers from poverty is supposed to drink. That he has 18s. or 20s. a week, and a family to bring up upon that income, is not considered evidence of want. People who have never spent less than £4 a week on themselves alone will declare that a clever managing woman can make 18s. or 20s. a week go as far as an ordinary woman, not a good manager, will make 30s. They argue as though the patent fact that 30s. misspent may reduce its value to 18s. could make 18s. a week enough to rear a family upon. It is not necessary to invoke the agency of drink to make 20s. a week too small a sum for the maintenance of four, five, six, or more, persons. That some men in possession of this wage may drink does not make it a sufficient wage for the families of men who do not drink.

It is now possible to begin calculations as to the expenditure of families of various sizes on a given wage or household allowance. For a family with six children the rent is likely to be 8s., 8s. 6d., or even 9s., for three or four rooms A woman with one or two children sometimes manages, by becoming landlady, to make advantageous arrangements with lodgers, and so reduce her payments, though not her risk, to considerably less than the usual market price of one or two fairly good rooms. But women with large families are not able to do this. A family with four or five children may manage in two rooms at a rental of 6s. to 7s., while a family with one, two, three or even occasionally four, children will take one room, paying from 3s. 6d. up to 5s., according to size. It is safe to assume that a man with a wife and six children and a wage of 24s. a week will allow 22s. for all outgoings other than his own clothes and pocket-money, and that his wife will pay for three, or perhaps four, rooms the sum of 8s. a week.

The budget may begin thus:

	s.	d.
Rent (four rooms: two upstairs, two down)	8	0
Clothing club	0	6
Boot club	1	0
Soap, soda, etc.	0	5
Burial insurance	0	11

The other regular items in such a woman's budget, apart from food, would be heating and lighting, comprising coal, wood, matches, gas or oil, and candles. The irregular items include doctor's visits to a sick child, which may cost 6d. a visit, or 1s. a visit, including medicine, and renewals which may be provided for by " crockery club, 4d.," or may appear as "teapot, 6d.," or "jug, 3¾d.," at rare intervals.

Coal is another necessary for which the poor pay a larger price than the well-to-do. The Lambeth woman is compelled to buy her coal by the hundredweight for two reasons, the chief of which is that she is never in possession of a sum of ready money sufficient to buy it by the ton or by the half-ton. A few women, in their passion for regular weekly payments, make an arrangement with the coalman to leave 1 cwt. of coal every week throughout the year, for which they pay a settled price. In the summer the coal, if they are lucky enough to have room to keep it, accumulates. One such woman came through the coal strike without paying anything extra. She used only ½ cwt. a week from the coalman, and depended for the rest upon her store. But not all have the power to do this, because they have nowhere to keep their coal but a box on the landing or a cupboard beside the fireplace. They therefore pay in an ordinary winter 1s. 6d. a cwt., except for any specially cold spell, when they may pay 1s. 7d. or 1s. 8d. for a short time; and in the summer they probably pay 8d. or 8½d. for ½ cwt. a week. In districts of London where the inhabitants are rich enough to buy coal by the ton, the same quality as is used in Lambeth can be bought in an ordinary winter— even now, when the price is higher than it used to be—for 22s. 6d. a ton, with occasional short rises to

23s. 6d. in very cold weather. Householders who have a large cellar space have been able to buy the same quality of coal which the Lambeth people burn, in truck loads, at the cheap time of year, at a price of about 20s. a ton. The Lambeth woman who buys by the hundredweight deems herself lucky. Only those in regular work can always do that. Some people, poorer still, are driven to buy it by the 14 lbs. in bags which they fetch home themselves. For this they pay a higher proportionate price still. While, therefore, it has been in the power of the rich man to buy cheap coal at £1 a ton, the poor man has paid 30s. a ton in winter, and almost 27s. in summer—a price for which the rich man could and did get his best quality silkstone.

Wood may cost 2d. a week, or in very parsimonious hands 1d. is made to do. Gas, by the penny-in-the-slot system, is used rather more for cooking than lighting. The expense in such a family as that under consideration would be about 1s.

The budget now may run:

					s.	d.
Rent ..	..	..	..	..	8	0
Clothing club		..	..	..	0	6
Boot club ..		..	..	..	1	0
Burial insurance		..	..	..	0	11
Coal ..	..	..	..	..	1	6
Gas ..	..	..	..	..	1	0
Wood	..	..	..	..	0	1
Cleaning materials	..		..	..	0	5
					13	5

The whole amount of the household allowance was supposed to be 22s. The amount left for food therefore would be 8s. 7d. in a week when no irregular and therefore extra expense, such as a doctor's visit or a new teapot, is incurred. This reasoned calculation of expenses other than food has been built up from the actual personal knowledge of the visitors in the investigation—from the study of rent-books and of insurance-books, from the sellers of coal, from the amount taken by the gasman from the meter, from the amount paid in clothing clubs and boot clubs, down to the price of soap and soda and wood at the local shop. It does not depend upon the budget or *bona fides* of any one woman. It is therefore given in order to show how closely it bears out budget after budget of woman after woman now to be given.

Mr. P., printer's labourer. Average wage 24s. Allows 20s. to 22s. Six children.

November 23, 1910, allowed 20s.

	s.	d.
Rent	8	0
Burial insurance (2d. each child, 3d. wife, 5d. husband; unusually heavy)	1	8
Boot club	1	0
Soap, soda, blue	0	4½
Wood	0	3
Gas	0	8
Coal	1	0
	12	11½

Left for food .. 7s. 0½d.

November 30, allowed 20s.

	s.	d.
Rent	8	0
Burial insurance	1	8
Boot club	1	0
Soap, soda, blue, starch	0	5
Gas	0	8
Coal	1	0
	12	9

Left for food .. 7s. 3d.

December 7, allowed 20s.

	s.	d.
Rent .. .. ∴	8	0
Burial insurance	1	8
Coal	1	6
Boot club	1	0
Soap, soda, etc.	0	5
Wood	0	3
Gas	1	0
Hearthstone and blacklead ..	0	1
Blacking	0	1
Cotton and tapes	0	3
	14	3

Left for food .. 5s. 9d.

A note in margin of this budget explains that no meat was bought that week owing to a present of a pair of rabbits. Meat generally cost 2s. 6d.

The next week Mr. P. was ill and earned only 19s. He allowed 18s. 1d.

	s.	d.
Rent	8	0
Burial insurance (stood over) ..	—	
Boot club	1	0
Coal	0	6
Liquorice-powder	0	1
Wood	0	2
Gas	0	9
	10	6

Left for food .. 7s. 7d.

6

This family spent extraordinarily little upon coal, and less than the usual amount on gas. Their great extravagance was in burial insurance. The extra penny on each child was not to bring a larger payment at death, but to provide a small sum at the age of fourteen with which to start the child in life. A regular provision of 6d. for other clothing than boots was made when the household allowance rose to 21s. 9d. on January 6, 1911.

Mr. B., printer's warehouseman, jobbing hand. Average wage 23s. Allows 20s. Four children.

August 18, 1910, allowed 20s.

	s.	d.
Rent	8	0
Burial insurance	1	0
Coal (regular sum paid all through the year)	1	6
Oil and wood	0	4½
Soap, soda, etc.	0	5½
	11	4

Left for food .. 8s. 8d.

August 25, work slack, allowed 18s.

	s.	d.
Rent	8	0
Coal	1	6
Burial insurance (left over) ..		—
Oil and wood..	0	4½
Soap, soda, etc.	0	5½
	10	4

Left for food .. 7s. 8d.

September 1, allowed 20s.

	s.	d.
Rent	8	0
Burial insurance (partly back payment)	1	6
Coal	1	6
Soap and soda	0	4½
Wood and oil	0	4½
	11	9

Left for food .. 8s. 3d.

September 8, allowed 20s.

	s.	d.
Rent	8	0
Burial insurance	1	0
Coal	1	6
Doctor (sick child)	1	0
Soap, soda, etc.	0	4½
Stamps	0	3
Oil and wood (extra light at night for illness)	0	6
	12	7½

Left for food .. 7s. 4½d.

This family make no regular provision for clothing of any kind. Overtime work solves the problem partly, and throughout the year the budgets show scattered items of clothing.

Mr. K., labourer. Wage 24s. Allows 22s. 6d. Six children.

March 23, 1911, allowed 22s. 6d.

	s.	d.
Rent	8	6
Burial insurance	1	0
Oil and candles	0	8
Coal	1	6
Clothing club	0	6
Soap, soda	0	5
Blacking and blacklead	0	1½
	12	8¼

Left for food .. 9s. 9½d.

March 30, allowed 22s. 6d.

					s.	d.
Rent ..	..	..	..	..	8	6
Burial insurance		..	..	..	1	0
Oil and candles		..	..	..	0	8
Clothing club		..	..	..	0	6
Soap, soda, etc.		..	..	..	0	5
Coal ..	..	..	..	..	1	6
Wood..	..	..	..	..	0	3
					12	10

Left for food .. 9s. 8d.

April 6, allowed 21s.

					s.	d.
Rent ..	..	..	..	..	8	6
Burial insurance	..	..	..	..	1	0
Coal ..	..	..	..	..	1	6
Clothing club (left over)		..	..	..	—	
Oil and candles		..	..	..	0	8
Soap, soda, etc.		..	..	..	0	5
					12	1

Left for food .. 8s. 11d.

No gas was laid on in the house. The item for coal, therefore, is moderate, as most women pay 1s. 6d. for 1 cwt. of coal a week in cold weather, besides paying 10d. or 1s. for gas. Boots are paid for when required. A note against the budget for April 13 says: " Sole old pram for 3s, it was to litle. Bourt boots for Siddy for 2s. 11½d. Made a apeny."

Mr. L., builder's handyman. Wage 23s. Allows 19s. to 20s. Six children alive.

July 10, 1912, allowed 19s. 6d.

	s.	d.
Rent (two upstairs rooms; lost one child)	6	6
Burial insurance	1	0
½ cwt. of coal	0	8½
Wood	0	2
Gas	0	6
Soap, soda, etc.	0	4
Blacking	0	1
Boracic powder	0	1
	9	4½

Left for food .. 10s. 1½d.

July 17, allowed 19s. 6d.

	s.	d.
Rent	6	6
Burial insurance	1	0
½ cwt. of coal	0	8½
Gas	0	6
Wood	0	2
Soap, soda	0	4
	9	2½

Left for food .. 10s. 3½d.

July 24, allowed 19s.

	s.	d.
Rent	6	6
Burial insurance	1	0
½ cwt. of coal	0	8½
Wood	0	2
Gas	0	6
Soap, soda	0	4
	9	2½

Left for food .. 9s. 9½d.

This family squeezes six children into two rooms, thereby saving from 1s. 6d. to 2s. a week, and makes no regular provision for clothing.

Clothes are partly paid for by extra money earned by Mr. L. in summer, when work is good.

Mr. S., scene-shifter. Wage 24s. Allows 22s. Six children alive.

October 12, 1911, allowed 22s.

	s.	d.
Rent (two very bad rooms, ground-floor; lost five children)	5	0
Burial insurance	2	0
½ cwt. of coal	0	8
Wood	0	2
Gas	0	6
Mr. T.'s bus fares	1	0
Newspaper	0	2
Soap, soda, etc.	0	5½
Boracic ointment	0	2
Gold-beater's skin	0	1
Collar	0	3
Pair of socks	0	4½
Boy's suit (made at home)	1	2
	12	0

Left for food .. 10s.

October 19, allowed 22s.

	s.	d.
Rent	5	0
Burial insurance	2	0
¾ cwt. of coal	1	0
Wood	0	2
Gas	0	8
Soap, soda	0	4
Bus fares	1	0
Newspaper	0	2
Children's Band of Hope (two weeks)	0	6
Mending boots	0	6
Material for dress	0	4½
Cotton and tape	0	3
	11	11½

Left for food .. 10s. 0½d.

October 26, allowed 22s.

	s.	d.
Rent	5	0
Burial insurance	2	0
½ cwt. of coal	0	8
Wood	0	1
Gas	0	3
Soap, soda	0	4½
Lamp oil	0	2
Matches	0	1
Bus fares	1	0
Newspaper	0	2
Children's Band of Hope	0	3
Mending boots	1	0
Print	0	6
Pair of stockings	0	4½
Boy's coat (made at home) ..	0	9
	12	8

Left for food .. 9s. 4d.

In this family there is no regular provision for clothes, which are paid for as they must be bought. No extra money is at any time of the year forthcoming. Mr. S. clothes himself, but extracts from his wife his newspaper as well as his fares. The latter are usually paid by the men. The mother is an excellent needlewoman, and makes nearly all the children's clothes. She is also a wonderful manager, and her two rooms are as clean as a new pin. This had not prevented her from losing five children when these particular budgets were taken. She soon after lost a sixth. The rent is far too low for healthy rooms. Though she pays for the same number of rooms as Mrs. L., she pays 1s. 6d. less a week for them, and they are wretchedly inferior. Her burial insurance is extremely high. Her record shows that she thought herself wise to make the sum so liberal. Even then she had to borrow 10s. to help to pay the 30s. for the funeral of her last child, because the burial insurance money only amounted to £1.

All the women, with the exception of Mrs. K., are notable managers, and all but Mrs. K. and Mrs. P. are extremely tidy and clean. Mrs. K., who has five sons and a daughter, is more happy-go-lucky than the others, as, fortunately for her, her husband " can't abide ter see the 'ouse bein' cleaned," and when it is clean " likes to mess it all up agen." Mrs. K. doesn't go in for worryin' the boys, either. Her eldest child is Louie, the only girl, who is thirteen, and rather good at school, but doesn't do much to help at home, as Mrs. K. likes to see her happy. With all her casual ways, Mrs. K. has a delicate mind, and flushes deeply if the visitor alludes to anything which shocks her. Louie's bed is shared by only one small brother; Louie's clothes are tidy, though Mr. and Mrs. K. seem to sleep among a herd of boys, and Mrs. K.'s skirt looks as though rats had been at it, and her blouse is never where it should be at the waist.

Mrs. P. is under thirty, and, when she has time to look it, rather pretty. Her eldest child is only ten. The tightest economy reigns in that little house, partly because Mr. P. is a careful man and very delicate, and partly because Mrs. P.

is terrified of debt. It was she who discovered
the plan of buying seven cracked eggs for 3d.
As she said, it might lose you a little of the egg,
but you could smell it first, which was a convenience. She is clean, but untidy, very gentle in
her manner, and as easily shocked as Mrs. K.
Her mother rents one of her rooms, and, much
beloved, is always there to advise in an unscientific, inarticulate, but soothing way when there is
a difficulty. The children are fair and delicate,
and are kept clean by their tired little mother,
who plaintively declared that she preferred boys
to girls, because you could cut their hair off and
keep their heads clean without trouble, and also
because their nether garments were less easily
torn. When in the visitor's presence the little
P.'s have swallowed a hasty dinner, which may
consist of a plateful of " stoo," or perhaps of
suet pudding and treacle, taken standing, they
never omit to close their eyes and say, " Thang
Gord fer me good dinner—good afternoon, Mrs.
R." before they go. Mrs. P. would call them all
back if they did not say that.

Mrs. B. is a manager who could be roused at
any moment in the night and inform the inquirer
exactly what money she had in her purse, and
how many teaspoonfuls of tea were left, before she
properly opened her eyes. She likes to spend
exactly the same sum on exactly the same article,
and the same amount of it, every week. Her
menus are deplorably monotonous—never a flight

into jam, when the cheapest " marge " goes
farther ! Never an exciting sausage, but always
stew of " pieces " on Wednesday and stew
warmed up on Thursday. When bread goes up
it upsets her very much. It gives her quite a
headache trying to take the exact number of
farthings out of other items of expenditure without upsetting her balance. She loved keeping
accounts. It was a scheme which fell in with the
bent of her mind, and, though she is no longer
visited, she is believed to keep rigorous accounts
still. She and all her family are delicate. Her
height is about 5 feet, and when the visitor
first saw her, and asked if Mr. B. were a big man,
she replied, " Very big, miss—'e's bigger than
me." She was gentle with children, and liked
to explain to a third person their constant and
mysterious symptoms. She dressed tidily, if
drably, and always wore a little grey tippet or a
man's cap on her head.

Mrs. L. is older and larger and more gaunt—a
very silent woman. Mr. L. talks immensely, and
takes liberties with her which she does not seem
to notice. She is gentle and always tidy, always
clean, and very depressed in manner. When her
baby nearly died with double pneumonia, she sat
up night after night, nursed him and did all the
work of the house by day, but all she ever said on
the subject was, " I'd not like ter lose 'im now."
She looked more gaunt as the days went on, but
everything was done as usual. When the baby

recovered she made no sign. Before marriage she had been a domestic servant in a West-End club, receiving 14s. a week and all found. Her savings furnished the home and bought clothes for some years.

Mrs. S. could tell you a little about Mr. S. if you pressed her. He was a " good 'usbin'," but not desirable on Saturday nights. She was a worn, thin woman with a dull, slow face, but an extraordinary knack of keeping things clean and getting things cheap. All her bread was fetched by her eldest boy of thirteen from the back door of a big restaurant once a week. It lived in a large bag hung on a nail behind the door, and got very stale towards the end of the week; but it was good bread. She could get about 100 broken rolls for 1s. 9d. When she lost her children she cried a very little, but went about much as usual, saying, if spoken to on the subject, " I done all I could. 'E 'ad everythink done fer 'im," which was perfectly true as far as she was concerned, and in so far as her means went. She loved her family in a patient, suffering, loyal sort of way which cannot have been very exhilarating for them.

All of these women, with, perhaps, the exception of Mrs. K., seemed to have lost any spark of humour or desire for different surroundings. The same surroundings with a little more money, a little more security, and a little less to do, was about the best their imaginations could grasp.

They knew nothing of any other way of living if
you were married. Mrs. K. liked being read to.
Her husband, hearing that she had had " Little
Lord Fauntleroy " read aloud to her at her
mothers' meeting, took her to the gallery of a
theatre, where she saw acted some version, or
what she took for some version, of this story. It
roused her imagination in a way which was
astonishing. She questioned, she believed, she
accepted. There were people like that! How
real and how thrilling! It seemed to take something of the burden of the five boys and the girl
from her shoulders. Did the visitor think theatres
wrong? No, the visitor liked theatres. Well,
Mrs. K. would like to go again if it could possibly
be afforded, but of course it could not. At the
mothers' meeting they were now having a book
read to them called " Dom Quick Sotty." It was
interesting, but not *so* interesting as " Little Lord
Fauntleroy," though, of course, that would be
Mrs. K.'s own fault most probably. Mrs. K.'s
criticism on " Mrs. Wiggs of the Cabbage Patch,"
later, was that it was a book about a queer sort of
people.

The children of these five families were, on the
whole, well brought up as regards manners and
cleanliness and behaviour. All of them were
kindly and patiently treated by their mothers.
Mrs. P., who was only twenty-eight, was a little
plaintive with her brood of six. Mrs. K., as has
been explained, was unruffled and placid. The

other three were punctual, clean, and gentle, if a
trifle depressing.   Want of the joy of life was the
most salient feature of the children as they grew
older.   They too readily accepted limitations and
qualifications imposed upon them, without that
irrational hoping against impossibility and belief
in favourable miracles which carry more fortunate
children through many disappointments.   These
children never rebel against disappointment.   It
is their lot.   They more or less expect it.   The
children of Mrs. K. were the most vital and noisy
and troublesome, and those of Mrs. B. the most
obedient and quiet, and what the women themselves called " old-fashioned."   All the children
were nice creatures, and not one of them was a
" first-class life " or gave promise of health and
strength.

NOTE.—In dissecting budgets in this and following
chapters the writer has not reckoned in the extra
nourishment which was provided for mother and child.
It is obvious that general calculations based upon such
temporary and unusual assistance would be misleading
with regard to the whole class of low-paid labour:

CHAPTER VII

FOOD: CHIEF ARTICLES OF DIET

WE now come to food. Two questions, besides
that of the amount of money to be spent, bear
upon food. What are the chief articles of diet ?
Where are they bought ? Without doubt, the
chief article of diet in a 20s. budget is bread. A
long way after bread come potatoes, meat, and
fish. Bread is bought from one of the abundance
of bakers in the neighbourhood, and is not as a
rule very different in price and quality from bread
in other parts of London. Meat is generally bargained for on street stalls on Saturday night or
even Sunday morning. It may be cheaper than
meat purchased in the West End, but is as certainly worse in original quality as well as less fresh
and less clean in condition. Potatoes are generally 2 lbs. for 1d., unless they are " new " potatoes.
Then they are dearer. When, at certain seasons
in the year, they are " old " potatoes, they are
cheaper; but then they do not "cut up " well,
owing to the sprouting eyes. They are usually
bought from an itinerant barrow. Bread in
Lambeth is bought in the shop, because the baker
is bound, when selling over the counter, to give

legal weight. In other words, when he is paid for
a quartern he must sell a quartern.   He therefore
weighs two "half-quartern" loaves, and makes
up with pieces of bread cut from loaves he keeps
by him for the purpose until the weight is correct.
In different districts bakers sell a quartern for
slightly different prices. The price at one moment south of Kennington Park may be 5d.,
while up in Lambeth proper it may be 5½d.   In
Kensington at the same moment delivered bread
is perhaps being sold at 6d. a quartern. The difference in price, therefore, at a given moment might
amount to as much as 7d. a week in the case of a
large family, and 3d. in the case of a small family.

When a weekly income is decreased for any
cause, the one item of food which seldom varies—
or at any rate is the last to vary—is bread.
Meat is affected at once. Meat may sink from
4s. a week to 6d. owing to a fluctuation in income.
But the amount of bread bought when the full
allowance was paid is, if possible, still bought
when meat may have almost decreased to nothing.
The amount of bread eaten in an ordinary
middle-class, well-to-do, but economically managed household of thirteen persons is 18 quarterns,
or 36 loaves, a week—something not far short of
3 loaves a head a week. This takes no heed of
innumerable cakes and sweet puddings consumed
by these thirteen persons, who at the same time
are consuming an ample supply of meat, fish,
bacon, fruit, vegetables, butter, and milk.

In Lambeth, the amounts spent on bread and meat respectively by the wives of four men in regular work are given below:

Mrs. D.: Allowance, 28s.; ten persons to feed; 10½ quartern at 5½d.; meat, 4s. 2d.

Mrs. C.: Allowance, 21s.; eight persons to feed; 8½ quartern at 5½d.; meat, 3s. 2½d.

Mrs. J.: Allowance, 22s.; five persons to feed; 7 quartern at 5½d.; meat, 2s. 11d.

Mrs. G.: Allowance, 19s. 6d.; five persons to feed; 5½ quartern at 5½d.; meat, 2s. 2d.

It will be seen that a quartern a head a week is the least amount taken in these four cases. On the whole, it would be a fairly correct calculation to allow this quantity as the amount aimed at as a minimum in most lower working-class families. The sum spent on meat may perhaps be greater than the sum spent on bread. But meat goes by the board before bread is seriously diminished, should the income suffer. This the three cases given here will show:

Mrs. W.: Allowance, 23s.; eight persons to feed; 9½ quartern; meat, 3s. 9½d.

Allowance reduced to 17s.; eight persons to feed ; 8½ quartern; meat, 1s. 6d.

Allowance reduced to 10s. (rent unpaid); eight persons to feed; 6 quartern; meat, 6d.

Mrs. S.: Allowance, 21s.; eight persons to feed; 7 quartern; meat, 2s. 6d.

Allowance reduced to 18s.; eight persons to feed; 7 quartern; meat, 1s. 2d.

Mrs. M.: Allowance, 20s.; six persons to feed; 7 quartern; meat, 2s. 10d.

Allowance reduced to 18s.; six persons to feed; 7 quartern; meat, 2s.

It is difficult to arrive at the quantity of meat, as it is often bargained for and sold by the piece without weighing. The experienced housewife offers so much, while the ticket on the meat is offering it for so much more. A compromise is arrived at and the commodity changes hands. " Pieces " are sold by weight, but are of various qualities and prices. Good " pieces " may be 6d. per lb., fair " pieces " are sold for 4½d., which is the most common price paid for them, but inferior " pieces " can be had for 3d. on occasions. They are usually gristle and sinew at that price.

Meat is bought for the men, and the chief expenditure is made in preparation for Sunday's dinner, when the man is at home. It is eaten cold by him the next day. The children get a pound of pieces stewed for them during the week, and with plenty of potatoes they make great show with the gravy.

Bread, however, is their chief food. It is cheap; they like it; it comes into the house ready cooked; it is always at hand, and needs no plate and spoon. Spread with a scraping of butter, jam, or margarine, according to the length of purse of the mother, they never tire of it as long as they are in their ordinary state of health. They receive it into their hands, and can please themselves as to where and how they eat it. It makes the sole article in the menu for two meals in the day. Dinner may consist of anything, from the joint on Sunday to boiled rice on

7

Friday. Potatoes will play a great part, as a rule, at dinner, but breakfast and tea will be bread.

Potatoes are not an expensive item in the 20s. budget. They may cost 1s. 3d. a week in a family of ten persons, and 4d. a week in a family of three. But they are an invariable item. Greens may go, butter may go, meat may diminish almost to the vanishing-point, before potatoes are affected. When potatoes do not appear for dinner, their place will be taken by suet pudding, which will mean that there is no gravy or dripping to eat with them. Treacle, or—as the shop round the corner calls it—" golden syrup," will probably be eaten with the pudding, and the two together will form a midday meal for the mother and children in a working man's family. All these are good—bread, potatoes, suet pudding; but children need other food as well.

First and foremost children need milk. All children need milk, not only infants in arms. When a mother weans her child, she ought to be able to give it plenty of milk or food made with milk. The writer well remembers a course of eloquent and striking lectures delivered by an able medical man to an audience of West-End charitable ladies. He ended his course by telling his audience that, if they wished to do good to the children of the poor, they would do more towards effecting their purpose if they were to walk through East End streets with placards bearing the legend " MILK is the proper food for infants," than by taking any other action he could think of. His audience was deeply interested and utterly believing. The fact that the children of the poor never taste milk once they cease to be nursed by their mothers was well known to the lecturer through his hospital experience, and hence his earnest appeal to have the mothers of those children taught what was the proper food to give them. He was, however, wrong in his idea that poor women do not realize that milk is the proper food for infants. The reason why the infants do not get milk is the reason why they do not get good housing or comfortable clothing—it is too expensive. Milk costs the same, 4d. a quart, in Lambeth that it costs in Mayfair. A healthy child ought to be able to use a quart of milk a day, which means a weekly milk bill for that child of 2s. 4d.—quite an impossible amount when the food of the whole family may have to be supplied out of 8s. or 9s. a week. Even a pint a day means 1s. 2d. a week, so that is out of the question, though a pint a day would not suffice for a child of a year old, who would need his or her full share of potatoes and gravy and bread as well. As it is, the only milk the children of the labourer get is the separated tinned milk, sold in 1d., 2d., 3d., and 4d. tins, according to size. These tins bear upon them in large red letters the legend, " This milk is not recommended as food for infants." The children do not get too much even of such milk. Families of ten

persons would take two tins at 3½d. in the week.
Families of five, six, or seven, would probably
take one such tin.   It is used to put in tea, which,
as it is extremely sweet, it furnishes with sugar as
well as with milk.   Sometimes it is spread on the
breakfast slice of bread instead of butter or jam.
An inexperienced visitor probably suggests that
it would make a good milk pudding, but is silenced
by hearing that it would take half a tin to make
one pudding, and then there is no richness in it.
Some people have suggested skim milk as a way
round this very terrible deprivation of the hard-
working poor.   But skim milk does not take the
place of whole milk as a food for infants. Parents
who are comfortably off would never dream of
starving their infants upon it.   Even supposing
that the children of the poor could magically
flourish upon skim milk alone, there is not enough
of it on the market to allow its use to be regarded
as a universal panacea for hungry babies.   In
fact, it is worth a moment's speculation as to
whether the whole milk-supply of England is
sufficient to insure a quart a day to each English
child under five years of age.   It is more than
likely that, unless the milk-supply were enor-
mously increased, adults would have to go entirely
without milk should the nation suddenly awake
to its duty towards its children.

The purpose of this book is not to inquire as to
whether this mother or that mother might not do
a little better than she does if she bought some

skim milk, or trained her children to enjoy burned porridge. It is to inquire whether, under the same conditions and with the same means at their command, any body of men or women could efficiently and sufficiently lodge and feed the same number of children.

A boys' home which maintains some thirty children between the ages of six and fifteen feeds, clothes, and lodges, each boy on an average of 6s. a week. This does not sound an extravagant sum. It is the outcome of much study, great knowledge of the subject, and untiring zeal. The working man's wife whose husband out of a 22s. or 23s. wage allows her 20s., and who has that convenient family of three children which is permitted by experts on the subject to be a becoming number in a working-class family, has only 4s. a head on which to feed, lodge, and clothe, the family.

Milk depots have been in existence in Lambeth for some years, and have undoubtedly done splendid service to babies under one year of age whose mothers cannot nurse them, but can afford to pay the growing amount of 9d. to 3s. a week for their children. The milk has to be called for, which limits the area in which it can be supplied; but it is sent out in sealed vessels, and is mixed in the exact proportions suitable to the age of the infant. So, when it can be afforded, its results are excellent. Unfortunately, the nursing mother is not helped by this, and it is she who requires milk for the needs of the baby she is nursing. Moreover, the price is, in the case of the 20s. budget, quite out of the question should the children number more than one, or at the most two·

As things are, once weaned, the child of a labouring man gets its share of the family diet. It gets its share of the 4d. tin of separated milk, its share of gravy and potatoes, a sip of the cocoa on which 3d. or 4d. a week may be spent for the use of everyone, and, if its father be particularly partial to it, a mouthful of fat bacon once or twice a week, spared from the not too generous " relish to his tea." Besides these extras it gets bread.

Women in the poorer working-class districts nurse their babies, as a rule, far longer than they should. It is not unusual for a mother to say that she always nurses until they are a year old. In many cases where a better-off mother would recognize that she is unable to satisfy her child's hunger, and would wean it at once, the poor mother goes hopelessly on because it is cheaper to nurse. It is less trouble to nurse, and it is held among them to be a safeguard against pregnancy. For those three reasons it is difficult to persuade a Lambeth woman to wean her child. In most of these cases milk or palatable food supplied to the mother would save the situation, and contrive a double debt to pay—the welfare of both mother and child. But the mother, who is by nature a poor nurse, usually finds, when she " gets about again," that her milk deserts her, and the grave difficulty of rearing the baby is met by her with a weekly 5d. tin of milk of a brand which has not been separated, but which is a very inádequate quantity for an infant.

The articles of diet other than bread, meat, potatoes (with occasional suet puddings and tinned milk), are fish, of which a shilling's worth may be bought a week, and of which quite half will go to provide the bread-winner with " relishes," while the other half may be eaten by the mother and children; bacon, which will be entirely consumed by the man; and an occasional egg. The tiny amounts of tea, dripping, butter, jam, sugar, and greens, may be regarded rather in the light of condiments than of food.

The diet where there are several children is obviously chosen for its cheapness, and is of the filling, stodgy kind.   There is not enough of anything but bread.   There is no variety.   Nothing is considered but money.

CHAPTER VIII

THE place where food is bought is important. How it is bought and when are also important questions. The usual plan for a Lambeth house-keeper is to make her great purchase on Saturday evening when she gets her allowance. She prob-ably buys the soap, wood, oil, tea, sugar, mar-garine, tinned milk, and perhaps jam, for the week. To these she adds the Sunday dinner, which means a joint or part of a joint, greens, and potatoes. The bread she gets daily, also the rasher, fish, or other relish, for her husband's special use. Further purchases of meat are made, if they are made, about Wednesday, while pota-toes and pot herbs, as well as fish, often come round on barrows, and are usually bought as re-quired. When she has put aside the rent, the insur-ance, the boot club money, and spent the Saturday night's five or six shillings, she keeps the pennies for the gas-meter and the money for the little extras in some kind of purse or private receptacle which lives within reach of her hand. A woman, during the time she is laid up at her confinement, will sleep with her purse in her hand or under the pillow, and during the daytime she doles out with an anxious heart the pennies for gas or the two-pences for father's relish. She generally complains bitterly that the neighbour who is " doing " for her has a heavy hand with the margarine, and no conscience with the tea or sugar.

The regular shopping is monotonous. The order at the grocer's shop is nearly always the same, as is also that at the oilman's. The Sunday dinner requires thought, but tends to repeat itself with the more methodical housewife, who has perhaps a leaning towards neck of mutton as the most interesting of the cheaper joints, or towards a half-shoulder as cutting to better advantage. It is often the same dinner week after week—one course of meat with greens and potatoes. Some women indulge in flights of fancy, and treat the family to a few pounds of fat bacon at 6d. per pound, a quality which is not to be recommended, or even to the extravagance of a rabbit and onions for a change. These women would be likely to vary the vegetables too; and in their accounts tomatoes, when tomatoes are cheap, may appear. It is only in the budgets of the very small family, however, that such extravagant luxuries would creep in.

In households where there is but one room there may be no storage space at all. Coal may be kept in the one cupboard on the floor beside the fireplace; or there may be such hoards of mice in the walls that no place is safe for food but a basin with a plate over it. One woman when lying in bed early in the morning unravelled a mystery which had puzzled her for weeks. She had not been able to find out how the food she kept on a high shelf of the dresser was being got at by mice. On the morning in question her eye was caught by movements which appeared to her to be in the air above her head. To her surprise, she realized that a long procession of mice was making use of her clothes-line to cross the room and climb down the loose end on to the high dresser shelf. They would, when satisfied, doubtless have returned by the same route had she not roused her husband. " But 'e ony terrified 'em," she said sadly, " 'e never caught one." In such cases it is necessary for the housekeeper to buy all provisions other than tinned milk, perhaps, day by day. She probably finds this more extravagant—even to the extent of paying more for the article. Tea, butter, and sugar, by the ounce may actually cost more, and they seldom go so far.

Another reason for buying all necessaries daily is that many men, though in a perfectly regular job (such as some kinds of carting), are paid daily, as though they were casuals. The amounts vary, moreover. One day they bring home 4s. 6d., another 3s. The housewife is never sure what she will have to spend, and as the family needs are, so must she supply necessaries out of the irregular daily sum handed to her.

The daily purchases of the wife of a dustsorter are given below. The husband was paid 3s. a day in cash, which he brought regularly to his wife. He collected out of the material he sorted, which came from the dustbins of Westminster, enough broken bread to sell as pig-food for a sum which paid both the rent and the burial insurance. He also collected and brought home each evening enough coal and cinders to supply the family needs, and, curiously enough, he collected and brought home a sufficiency of soap. After paying 5s. for rent and 1s. for insurance, he had enough left from these extra sources of income for his own pocket-money. With rent, insurance, coal, and soap, provided, the housekeeper would have been well off indeed, as Lambeth goes, could she have laid out her money to better advantage. She never had more than 3s. at a time, and was accustomed to buy everything day by day. There was but one room. There were four children, who looked stronger than they were. The mother suffered from anæmia, and was not a particularly good manager, though she fed her children fairly well and seemed to be a moderately good cook. She had no oven. An account of how she laid out her 18s. is given on pp. 108, 109.

It is obvious that this is an extravagant way of buying. Not only is the woman charged more for some items, such as sugar and butter, which she prefers to margarine even at the extra price,

but the daily purchase leads to larger amounts
being used. Her husband is a teetotaller, but
likes strong tea, and that very sweet. Hence
12 ozs. of tea, 3 lbs. of sugar, and 3 tins of milk.
The baby was very young and the mother anæmic,
and the 8d. for a girl to take it out is money use-
fully spent. Otherwise the infant would hardly
ever have left the room, as her mother does the

Monday, 3s.:

	s.	d.
2 ozs. tea, 2d.; ½ lb. sugar, 1½d.; 4 ozs. butter, 3½d.; bread, 3d.	0	10
Potatoes, 2d.; onions, carrots, greens, 2½d.	0	4½
Gas	0	2
	1	4½
In hand	1	7½

Tuesday, 3s.:

2 ozs. tea, 2d.; ½ lb. sugar, 1½d.; 4 ozs. butter, 3½d.; bread, 3d. ..	0	10
One tin of milk, 3½d.; relish for husband's tea, 2d.	0	5½
Potatoes, 2d.; greens and pot herbs, 3½d.; meat, 7d.	1	0½
Gas	0	2
	2	6
In hand	2	1½

Wednesday, 3s.:

2 ozs. tea, 2d.; ½ lb. sugar, 1½d.; 4 ozs. butter, 3½d.; bread, 3d.	0	10
1 lb. pieces, 4½d.; potatoes, 2d.; vegetables, 1½d.; rice, ½d.	0	8½
Clothing club	1	0
Gas	0	1
	2	7½
In hand	2	6

daily marketing when the baby is asleep. Since this account was made out the authorities have advised the family to take two rooms at an advanced rental of 2s., of which the father and mother each pay half. So the weekly list of purchases has now to be made out of 17s. The

Thursday, 3s.:

		s.	d.
½ lb. sugar, 1½d.; 4 ozs. butter, 3½d.; bread, 3d.		o	8
One tin of milk, 3½d.; meat, 6d.; potatoes, 2d.; Quaker oats, 2½d.; rice, ½d.		1	2½
Boot club		1	o
Gas		o	1
		2	11½
In hand		2	6½

Friday, 3s.:

		s.	d.
2 ozs. tea, 2d.; ½ lb. sugar, 1½d.; 4 ozs. butter, 3½d.; bread, 3d.		o	10
Suet, 2d.; flour, 2½d.; treacle, 1½d. ..		o	6
Gas		o	2
Five days' pay for neighbour's girl to take out the baby		o	6
		2	0
In hand		3	6½

Saturday, 3s. + 3s. 6½d. = 6s. 6½d.:

		s.	d.
2 ozs. tea, 2d.; ½ lb. sugar, 1½d.; 4 ozs. butter, 3½d.; bread, 6d.		1	1
One tin of milk, 3½d.; bacon, 6d.; eggs, 2d.; potatoes, 2d.; greens, 2d.		1	3½
Gas		o	1
Sunday's joint		2	0
Bakehouse		o	2
Blacklead, hearthstone, matches, soda ..		o	4
Husband's shirt		1	0
Baby's birth certificate		o	3
Girl to mind baby		o	2
		6	6½

baby is six months old instead of five weeks, and the mother's milk has completely failed her. Thus the expenses increase, while the housekeeping allowance is less.

In the case of women who handle the whole week's wage at once, there is generally great need of more cupboard space. Occasionally a scullery helps to solve the problem, and there is often a very shallow cupboard beside the chimney, high enough from the floor to be clear of mice and beetles, and out of reach of children. A kitchen with the copper in it is a bad place for keeping food; a kitchen infested with any kind of vermin is also a bad place to keep food; a kitchen which is plagued with flies is equally impossible. The women whose lives are passed in such kitchens may feel that, in spite of the extra expense and waste, daily buying of perishable food is a necessity.

A woman with a sick child—one of six—living in one room, was allowed milk for the use of the child, who was extremely ill. The only place where she could keep the milk was a basin with an old piece of wet rag thrown over it. The visitor found seven flies in the milk, and many others crawling on the inner side of the rag. The weather was stifling. The room, though untidy, was tolerably clean. But over the senseless child on the one bed in the room hovered a great cloud of flies. The mother stood hour after hour brushing them away. On the advice of the visitor the sick child was carried off there and then to the infirmary, where it ultimately recovered. Once the child was removed, the flies ceased to swarm into the room.

Cooking, which has already been mentioned in connection with old and burnt saucepans and utensils, is necessarily very perfunctory and rudimentary. To boil a neck with pot herbs on Sunday, and make a stew of "pieces" on Wednesday, often finishes all that has to be done with meat. The intermediate dinners will ring the changes on cold neck, suet pudding, perhaps fried fish or cheap sausages, and rice or potatoes. Breakfast and tea, with the exception of the husband's relishes, consist of tea, and bread spread with butter, jam, or margarine. In houses where no gas is laid on, the gas-stove cannot take the place of a missing oven, and it is extraordinary how many one-roomed dwellings are without an oven. Two pots, both burned, a frying-pan, and a kettle, do not make an equipment with which it is easy to manage the delicacies of cooking. Boiling can be done in a burnt saucepan, provided there is water enough in the can which stands behind the door to fill the pot sufficiently. Frying is held to be easy, but fat is not plentiful, and frying in Lambeth usually means frizzling in a very tiny amount of half-boiling grease. The great panful of fat which would be used by a good cook is impossible of attainment. To stand by and watch the cooking is difficult when so many things have to be done at once. The pot, once placed on the fire or the gas-stove, has to look after itself, while the mother nurses a baby, or does a bit of washing, or tidies the room and gets out the few plates which she calls " laying the dinner." The children all come trooping in from school before she has finished, and have to be scolded a little and told to get out of the way, and when she has got them arranged sitting or standing round the table she helps each one as quickly and fairly as she can. If her husband is not there, she may put aside his portion to be warmed up and eaten later. She does not attempt to eat with the family. She is server and provider, and her work is to see that everyone gets a fair share, according to his or her deserts and the merits of the case. She may or may not sit down, but perhaps with the baby in her arms she feeds the youngest but one with potato and gravy or suet pudding, whichever is the dinner of the day, for fear it shall waste its food and spoil its clothes. When the family have finished what she sets before them, she sees to washing of hands where the age of the washer is tender, and thankfully packs them all off again to afternoon school, having as likely as not called back the one who banged the door to tell him to go out again and " do it prop'ly." The husband may not like his dinner put aside for him, in which case a second cooking is necessary. So much has to be done each day. The Lambeth woman has no joy in cooking for its own sake.

CHAPTER IX

ACTUAL MENUS OF SEVERAL WORKING MEN'S FAMILIES

THE following is a week's menu taken from Mrs. X., the wife of a carter. His wages vary between 19s. and 23s. 6d., according to hours worked. In a Bank Holiday week they went down to 15s. He usually keeps 1s. a week, and has his dinners at home. There are four children, all under five. The rent is 4s. 6d. for one room. They do not insure, and are slightly in debt. Mrs. X. is a good manager. This menu was taken from a week when Mrs. X. had 22s. 6d. given her by her husband:

Sunday.—Breakfast: One loaf, 1 oz. butter, ½ oz. tea, a farthing's-worth of tinned milk, a half-pennyworth of sugar. Kippers extra for Mr. X. Dinner: Hashed beef, batter pudding, greens, and potatoes. Tea: Same as breakfast, but Mr. X. has shrimps instead of kippers.

Monday.—Breakfast: Same as Sunday. Mr. X. has a little cold meat. Dinner: Sunday's dinner cold, with pickles, or warmed up with greens and potatoes. Tea: One loaf, marmalade, and tea. Mr. X. has two eggs.

Tuesday.—Breakfast: One loaf, 1 oz. butter, two pennyworth of cocoa. Bloaters for Mr. X. Dinner: Bread and dripping, with cheese and tomatoes. Tea: One loaf, marmalade, and tea. Fish and fried potatoes for Mr. X.

Wednesday.—Breakfast: One loaf, 1 oz. butter, tea. Corned beef for Mr. X. Dinner: Boiled bacon, beans, and potatoes. Tea: One loaf, 1 oz. butter, and tea. Cold bacon for Mr. X.

Thursday.—Breakfast: One loaf, jam, and tea. Dinner: Mutton chops, greens, and potatoes. Tea: One loaf, 1 oz. butter, and tea.

Friday.—Breakfast: One loaf, 1 oz. butter, and tea. Dinner: Sausages and potatoes. Tea: One loaf, jam, and tea.

Saturday.—Breakfast: One loaf, 1 oz. butter, two pennyworth of cocoa. Dinner: Pudding of "pieces," greens, and potatoes. Tea: One loaf, 1 oz. butter, and tea. Fish and fried potatoes for Mr. X.

These children look fairly well and seem vigorous. The baby is being nursed. The other three live chiefly on bread, with potatoes and greens and a tiny portion of meat at dinner.

The budget of the whole expenses of this family for a week, though not necessarily for the same week as that of the menu, is given on p. 115.

Mr. Y. is a builder's handyman, whose wages average about 25s. a week. He allows as a rule 22s. 6d. to his wife, out of which she gives him back 3s. a week for his dinners when at work. There are six children under thirteen. The rent for two rooms upstairs is 6s. 6d., and burial insurance is 1s.

Sunday.—Breakfast: One loaf, jam, and tea. Bloater for him. Dinner: Half shoulder of mutton, greens, potatoes, and suet pudding, for all. Tea: Bread, butter, and tea.

Monday.—Breakfast: Bread, dripping, and tea. Cold meat from Sunday for him. Dinner for mother and children: Cold meat and potatoes over from Sunday. Tea: Bread, jam, and tea.

Tuesday.—Breakfast: Bread, dripping, and tea, for all. Dinner for mother and children: Hashed meat over from Monday and potatoes. Tea: Bread, radishes, and tea.

	s.	d.		s.	d.
Rent	4	6	12 loaves	2	9
1½ cwt. coal ..	2	0	1 lb. butter ..	1	2
Gas	1	6	8 ozs. tea	0	8
Soap, soda, blue ..	0	2	4 lbs. sugar ..	0	8
Clothing club ..	0	6	1 tin of milk ..	0	4
Paid off debt ..	1	0	¼ lb. cocoa	0	4
			6 lbs. meat ..	2	6
	9	8	12 lbs. potatoes ..	0	6
			Greens and pot herbs	0	5
			1 lb. currants ..	0	3
			1 quartern flour ..	0	6
			Suet	0	2
			1 lb. bacon ..	0	8
			Jam	0	4
			Fish	0	6
			Sausages	0	7
			Dripping	0	4
			Cheese	0	2
				12	10

Wednesday.—Breakfast: Bread, dripping, and tea. Dinner for mother and children: Dumplings in yesterday's gravy. Tea: Bread, jam, and tea, for all.

Thursday.—Breakfast: Bread, dripping, and tea. Dinner for mother and children: Rice and treacle. Tea: Bread, jam, and tea.

Friday.—Breakfast: Bread, jam, and tea. Dinner for mother and children: Barley broth and potatoes. Tea: Bread, dripping, and tea.

Saturday.—Breakfast: Bread, dripping, and tea. Dinner for mother and children: ¾ lb. sausages and potatoes. Tea: Bread, jam, and tea.

One of Mrs. T.'s weekly budgets is here given:

	s.	d.		s.	d.
Rent	6	6	Husband's dinners	3	0
Insurance ..	1	0	14 loaves	3	4½
Gas	0	6	1 lb. dripping ..	0	6
½ cwt. coal ..	0	8½	12 ozs. butter ..	0	9
Wood	0	2	8 ozs. tea ..	0	8
Soap, soda, blue,			2 tins of milk ..	0	6
starch	0	5	Meat	2	3
Boracic powder ..	0	1	6 lbs. potatoes ..	0	3
Baby's soap ..	0	2	Vegetables ..	0	6
			½ quartern flour ..	0	3
	9	6½	Bloaters	0	3
			Suet	0	2
			3 lbs. sugar ..	0	6
				12	11½

It will be noticed in this menu that Mr. T. gets no relish for either tea or breakfast throughout the week, with the exception of his Sunday treat. His 6d. dinner cannot be of a heavy nature, and his share of the family breakfasts and teas would in no way make up for a scanty dinner. He is not, therefore, too well fed. His wife and six children, who manage upon the dinners given in the menu, obviously do not get sufficient nourishment. This woman is an excellent cook, but her equipment is poor. She keeps her two rooms as clean as a new pin, and is punctual and methodical to a fault. But she is worn and tired, and unable to take in new ideas. The children are fairly well, but nervous and restless. They are not up to the normal size for their age, nor are they intelligent for their years. They are docile and give no trouble at school, and are considered " well brought up " by all who come into contact with them.

The following menu is that of the woman whose daily expenditure of 3s. a day is given in a previous chapter. Her husband, it will be remembered, pays rent and insurance, and brings home from his dust-heaps a sufficiency of fuel and soap. It is, unfortunately, not the menu of the week of which the expenditure is given. Mr. Z. allows his wife 3s. a day. There are four children under six. The rent of the one room is 5s. 6d.

Sunday.—Breakfast: Half a loaf of bread, butter, and tea. Dinner: Roast mutton, potatoes, and greens (5d.). Tea: Half a loaf of bread, butter, and tea; 2d. cake for him.

Monday.—Breakfast: Half a loaf of bread, rolled oats with tinned milk. Dinner: Cold meat cooked up with onions, carrots, greens, and potatoes. Tea: Half a loaf of bread, jam, and tea.

Tuesday.—Breakfast: Half a loaf of bread, jam, and tea. Dinner: Mutton chops, potatoes, and greens. Tea: Half a loaf of bread, butter, and tea; fish for him.

Wednesday.—Breakfast: Half a loaf of bread, butter, and cocoa. Dinner: Stew 1 lb. pieces ($4\frac{1}{2}$d.), with rice, carrots, onions, and potatoes. Tea: Half a loaf of bread, butter, and tea; fish for him.

Thursday.—Breakfast: Half a loaf of bread, tea, rolled oats and tinned milk. Dinner: Boiled neck, with potatoes, onions, rice, and greens. Tea: Half a loaf of bread, butter, and tea; fish for him.

Friday.—Breakfast: Half a loaf of bread, butter, and tea. Dinner: Suet pudding and treacle. Tea: Half a loaf of bread, jam, and tea.

Saturday.—Breakfast: Half a loaf of bread, butter, and tea. Dinner: Eggs (5d.) and bacon (3d.). Tea: Half a loaf of bread, butter, and tea.

It has already been admitted that Mrs. Z. is not such a good manager as most of the women dealt with in this investigation. She had two special difficulties to struggle with. Her husband's trade caused him to return home with clothes and skin almost equally black. He had no chance of a bath in the one room, and her instincts in the direction of cleanliness—whatever they may once have been—had evidently wilted in an unsympathetic atmosphere. Moreover, his hours were very irregular, and he was often a great deal at home in the afternoon. The daily payments were another stumbling-block, and there was no absolute certainty that the sum received would be 3s. Occasionally it was 2s., and sometimes it was only 1s. 6d. On one never-to-be-forgotten occasion when the visitor was present it was nothing at all, owing to his having arrived at work too late. These two influences certainly caused Mrs. Z. to be somewhat of a sloven; as she said: " It was rather funny gettin' accustomed ter sleepin' with 'im—all black like that." And all the time Mr. Z. is a most excellent husband, with a great admiration for his nice-looking wife. Mr. Z. never seemed to ail. He was a small man, and very muscular for his height. Mrs. Z., though anæmic, was a well-made, upright young woman, who was rather proud of her pretty figure. The four children were big and fat and fairly intelligent. They seemed thoroughly satisfactory until the eldest boy started " wastin' "— a process Lambeth children are given to embarking upon. He " wasted " and grew visibly thinner, to the complete bewilderment, according to Mrs. Z., of the " mission " doctor and the hospital doctor, to whom she took him. Both parents were overcome with alarm and sorrow, and the day that Ernie turned and took his food again was a day of great rejoicing. He never seemed to be so strong again, however, and the obstinate continuance of a bad form of eczema upon all the other three children, in spite of every kind of treatment by doctor and district nurse, points to a worse state of health than seemed at first to obtain amongst them. Mrs. Z. was a very affectionate mother, and prided herself on the fact that her four children were " a sight bigger for their age " than all the others in the street.

The next menu is that of Mrs. O., whose husband is a printer's labourer. He earns 30s. a week, and at Christmas he works overtime, which enables him, by working very long hours, to earn an irregular amount of extra money. Out of this he buys the children, of whom there are eight, their boots for the year, and some part of their clothing.

Sunday.—Breakfast: Fish all round, loaf of bread, margarine, 2 teaspoonfuls of tea, 4½ teaspoonfuls of tinned milk, small spoonful of sugar each.   Dinner: 3½ lbs. meat (1s. 9d.), greens, and potatoes; very occasionally a suet pudding.   Tea: Tea, bread, margarine, and watercress (½d.).

Monday.—Breakfast: Tea, bread, and margarine; rasher for him.   Dinner: Cold meat and vegetables left from Sunday.   Tea is bread and margarine every day in the week.

Tuesday.—Breakfast: Tea, bread, and margarine; haddock for him.   Dinner: Baked breast of mutton (7½d.), greens, and potatoes.

Wednesday.—Breakfast: Tea, bread, and margarine; rasher for him. Dinner: Stew of " pieces," pot herbs, and potatoes.

Thursday.—Breakfast: Tea, bread, and margarine; fish for him (2d.). Dinner: 1 lb. sausages (5d.) and potatoes; ½ lb. " skirt " of beef for him.

Friday.—Breakfast: Tea, bread, and margarine; rasher for him (2d.). Dinner: Fried strips of breast of mutton (4½d.) and potatoes; two chops for him (5d.).

Saturday.—Breakfast: Tea, bread, and margarine; fish for him (2d.). Dinner: 1 lb. pork chops (9½d.), four to a pound; he has one. Other three divided among seven children, with potatoes. She has an egg later. Supper: 6 ozs. cold meat from cookshop, with a lettuce for him. If any over she has some.

The mother here is a tall, well-made woman, and the father, who has been a soldier and went all through the South African War, is also of decent proportions. The children, however, are stunted, particularly the younger ones. They are sharp and intelligent, and very well behaved. They are not often ill, except for the usual visitations of measles and whooping-cough, but their eyes need close attention, which their mother religiously and painstakingly gives them daily. Two of them have been operated on for adenoids, and the third youngest, who is three, is no larger than a baby of one year, owing to a feeble and ailing babyhood. Both parents are specially attached to this child, who gave the mother bad nights for two years, and has needed incessant care and attention ever since her birth. The two boy babies, of two years and six months respectively, both terribly undersized, are far less noticed and petted than this delicate little girl of three whose life has always hung on a thread.

An interesting menu and budget is that of the Q.'s. He is a feather-cleaner's assistant, and his wages are 25s., out of which he allows 20s. to his wife, and keeps 5s. for himself. There are two children. They pay 6s. for the rent of two rooms. Mrs. Q. is a hard-working woman, a good manager, and extremely intelligent. The chief interest in this menu is that Mrs. Q. shows the way in which the little income is divided. Besides keeping 5s. a week for his own clothing and pocket-money, Mr. Q. has 6½d. a day allowed him by his wife for his dinners on six days a week when he is at work. Moreover, he demands 1s. 1d. to be spent weekly on himself alone for relishes at breakfast or tea. The income works out as given on p. 123.

The menu runs thus: Throughout the week every breakfast for mother and children consists of their shares in half a loaf of bread, with a touch from the weekly six pennyworth of margarine. This is accompanied by tea made from the 4 ozs. which has to last for seven days. The 2d. tin of milk and the 2 lbs. of sugar, which also have to do seven days' duty, furnish the tea with milk and sugar. The husband's relish at breakfast usually takes the shape of an egg.

Sunday.—Dinner is roast mutton, greens, and potatoes. Tea is tea, made as above, and toast. All the week-day teas for mother and children are a repetition of breakfast. Mr. Q. has fish or a rasher added.

The week-day dinners run thus:

Monday.—Cold mutton left from Sunday.

Tuesday.—Cold mutton left from Monday.

Wednesday.—Stew of ½ lb. " pieces " (2¼d.) and potatoes.

Mr. Q.'s Expenses.

	s.	d.
Kept by Mr. D. ..	5	0
His week-day din-ners	3	3
Relishes	1	1
	9	4

General Expenses.

	s.	d.
Rent	6	0
Coal	1	8
Gas	1	0
Soap, etc. ..	0	4½
Insurance ..	0	6
	9	6½

General Food shared by Mr. Q.

	s.	d.
Bread	2	1½
1 lb. margarine ..	0	6
4 ozs. tea	0	4
1 tin of milk ..	0	2
2 lbs. sugar ..	0	5
Sunday potatoes	0	2
Sunday greens ..	0	2
Suet	0	1
Sunday joint ..	1	0
	4	11½

Food not shared by Mr. Q. —Week-day Dinners of Mrs. Q. and Children.

	s.	d.
Meat	1	0
Potatoes	0	2
	1	2

Thursday.—Meat pudding from other ½ lb. of "pieces" (2¼d.) and potatoes.

Friday.—Liver (3d.), one rasher (1½d.), and potatoes.

Saturday.—Two herrings (3d.).

The sad part of these menus is that, though on paper it looks very selfish of Mr. Q., in practice his share of the half-loaf, even though accompanied by an egg, does not seem a very satisfactory or over-luxurious breakfast for a working man. His daily dinner at 6½d. cannot be an oppressive meal, whilst his tea cannot be much more satisfying than his breakfast. And yet, in order to feed him as well as this, his wife has to make about a third of the amount do for herself. It is not usual to find the accounts kept in this manner, but Mrs. Q. chose to show how the money went. As a matter of fact, except for the 5s. which Mr. Q. keeps for himself—a sum greater than that which is usually retained by the husband—the arrangements of the menu are quite ordinary.

The next menu is that of Mrs. U., whose husband drives a mail-van at night. His wages are 25s. a week, and he allows his wife 21s. Out of the 4s. kept by him, the usual 4d. goes in National Health Insurance, 6d. in a sick club, 1d. to the hospital, 1d. to the mess-room, and 6d. to his trade union. He is fed entirely at home. Mrs. U. has a daughter of fourteen, who goes out to daily work and is fed at home. She earns 4s.

a week, and brings it home regularly to her
mother. Thus the housekeeping allowance is
25s. a week. Mrs. U. bakes at home in the gas-
oven, at the cost in gas of about 6d. a week, and
for flour and yeast of 4s. 7d. The item for bread
is therefore high, but so also is the quality of
the bread. There are six children.

Most breakfasts and teas in the week consist
of bread, margarine, tea, cocoa, or coffee, or
occasionally of porridge and treacle.

Sunday.—Dinner: Target of mutton (10d.),
potatoes, greens, suet pudding, and haricot beans.

Monday.—Dinner: Boiled neck (4d.), potatoes,
and dumplings.

Tuesday.— Dinner: Stew of " pieces " (4d.)
with pot herbs and potatoes.

Wednesday.—Dinner: Brown hash (4d.) and
dumplings.

Thursday.—Dinner: Meat pudding of shin of
beef (4d.), greens, and potatoes.

Friday.—Dinner: Fish (1 lb., 4d.), parsley
sauce, and potatoes.

Saturday.—Dinner: Liver (4d.), bacon (2d.),
greens, and potatoes.

A week's budget of Mrs. U. is given on p. 126.

Mrs. U. is an excellent manager, and certainly
tries to feed her family well. But her plans are
sadly interfered with when one of the children
needs new boots, and, with six children, one or
other of them is always needing something new.
There are two courses which are taken according

to the merits of the case. One is to pawn the mother's boots, thus rendering her a prisoner in the two tiny rooms until the money to release her belongings can be raised, and the other is to save the amount out of food. She makes all the clothes that can be made at home, and is an expert needlewoman. She was a professed cook earning £1 a week before she married. No burial insurance is paid in this family.

	s.	d.		s.	d.
Rent	7	0	Flour and yeast ..	4	7
Gas	1	6	Meat ..	2	6
1½ cwt. coal	2	1½	Suet ..	0	3
Soap, soda	0	2	Potatoes ..	1	0
			Vegetables	0	6
	10	9½	2 lbs. margarine	1	0
			3 lbs. sugar	0	7
			Bacon ..	0	2
			6 ozs. tea ..	0	6
			Cocoa ..	0	3
			Coffee ..	0	3
			Fish ..	0	4
			Rice ..	0	2
			Split peas ..	0	2½
			Currants ..	0	2
			Lard ..	0	4
			Oatmeal ..	0	2½
			Treacle ..	0	1½
			Salt and pepper ..	0	2
			Cow's milk ..	0	8
			Eggs ..	0	3
				14	2½

We now come to the week's menu of a couple of families where the man was temporarily out of work, and took anything he could get. Mr. T. was carman for a large firm that employed all its enormous number of carmen by the day. The inner ring of men were given a day's work every day, and earned 3s. 6d., which they were paid on leaving work each night. The less fortunate outer ring were given a couple or three days' work in the week. No notice was taken or given on either side. A day's work might mean at Christmas time a day of twenty hours, and no meal-time allowed. It might mean a much shorter day, but usually ran about twelve hours. Mr. T. had two days' work a week, but he washed down another man's van every day for 1s. 6d. a week. Occasionally he was lucky enough to have two vans to wash, when his money would amount to 10s. He allowed his wife 8s. 6d. There was one child. The rent for the single room was 3s. 6d., and there was no insurance.

Sunday.—Breakfast: Bloater for father, 1 teaspoonful of tea between them, 1 teaspoonful of milk from tin each, 1 small spoonful of sugar each, two slices of bread and margarine. Dinner: Six pennyworth of neck of mutton, greens and potatoes given by mother. Tea: Two slices of bread, margarine, and tea.

Monday.—Breakfast: Two slices of bread and butter, with tea, for every breakfast in the week. Dinner: Cold meat and vegetables left from Sunday. Tea: Two slices of bread and butter, with tea, for every tea in the week.

Tuesday.—Dinner: Fresh herring each, bread and butter (one slice).

Wednesday.—Dinner: ½ lb. " pieces " (3d.) stewed with potatoes, which were given by mother.

Thursday.—Dinner: What is left of stew and potatoes.

Friday.—Dinner: ½ lb. rashers (3d.), with potatoes given by mother.

Saturday.—Dinner: The other ½ lb. rashers, with potatoes given by mother.

A week's budget runs thus:

	s.	d.		s.	d.
Rent	3	6	9 loaves	2	0¾
Gas	0	5	4 ozs. tea	0	4
Newspaper ..	0	1	1 lb. sugar ..	0	2
Candle	0	0¼	1 tin of milk ..	0	3
Soap, 1d.; soda, ½d.	0	1½	4 ozs. butter ..	0	3½
Blacklead ..	0	0½	1½ lbs. meat ..	0	9
Paid off cradle ..	0	6			
	4	8¼		3	10¼

It will be noticed that no coal appears. The time of year was summer, and the fire was never lighted during the thirteen weeks of their life on 8s. 6d. a week. The five pennyworth of gas was used entirely for cooking, and light was supplied by the farthing candle. The newspaper was their Sunday treat, and was read solemnly through from first column to last by both young people. It chronicled more murders and multiple births than any paper the visitor had ever seen. Mrs. T. would say in course of polite conversation: " Have you seen the news—five at a birth ?" Then she would produce a picture of three nurses and two doctors, each holding a baby, and would murmur regretfully: " They're most of 'em dead."

The next case is that of a Mrs. X., a deserted wife, with three children under eight. Mrs. X. had "taken the law of" Mr. X., and there was "an order out against him" for 7s. a week. But as she was never able to make him pay it or any part of it, she had to exist with the three children on her earnings as an office cleaner in a large bank in the city, where she was paid 12s. a week. Unfortunately the bank was very far from her home, and she spent 2s. a week on fares, which sounds very extravagant, but it must be remembered that she went to her work twice a day. Her hours were six to nine in the mornings, and six in the evenings until finished. She rented a small room for 2s. 6d. a week until the sanitary authorities found her out, and obliged her to move into two smaller rooms at a rent of 4s. 6d. Owing to her lack of beds and bedding she and her three children were forced to sleep all in one bed in one of the two smaller rooms exactly as they did when she had but the one larger room. To mind the baby of two while she was at work morning and evening she paid a neighbour 1s. a week. Added to her regular wage of 12s. as office cleaner, she occasionally had a job on Saturdays, which brought her in 1s. more, so that her income sometimes amounted to 13s. a week.

Her menu ran as follows:

Sunday.—Breakfast: Half a loaf, margarine, and tea. Dinner: Sausages, 1 lb. (4d.), or "pieces" (4d.), potatoes, sometimes pot herbs,

9

sometimes greens. Tea: Half a loaf, margarine, and tea.

Every breakfast and every tea in the week is half a loaf, dripping or margarine, and tea.

Monday.—Dinner: Remains of sausages and potatoes.

Tuesday.—Dinner: Flour pancakes, with sugar.

Wednesday.—Dinner: ¼ lb. bacon, half a loaf of bread.

Thursday.—Dinner: halfpennyworth of fish for Lulu, and halfpennyworth of potatoes. Landlord downstairs gave Mrs. X. some meat pie and potatoes.

Friday.—Dinner: Bread, margarine, and tea.

Saturday.—Dinner: Bread and three bloaters.

The following is a week's budget:

	s.	d.		s.	d.
Rent	4	6	6 loaves ..	1	10
Baby minded	1	0	2 lb. sugar	0	4
Fares	2	0	1 tin of milk	0	2
Coal	0	6¾	4 lbs. potatoes	0	2
Lamp oil ..	0	2	Flour	0	2
Wood	0	2	Meat and fish	0	4
Matches	0	0½	4 ozs. tea ..	0	4
Soap, soda, blue	0	2¼	Dripping ..	0	3
Sickness insurance	0	3	Margarine	0	0¾
Burial insurance	0	3	Oatmeal ..	0	3
	9	1¼		3	10¾

The eldest boy of seven has dinners at school five days in the week in term-time. The girl is three and a half, and is fed at home. The baby is two years old. All the children are extremely delicate. Since this menu was taken Mrs. X.

has been lucky enough to get help from some kind people. They have seen her elder boy through an attack of rheumatic fever, and have clothed the three children in warm and decent garments. Without such timely help she would in all probability have lost her boy.

There are those who, if they happen to read these weekly menus, will criticise with deep feeling the selection of the materials from which they are composed. It is not necessary to pretend that they are the absolute best that could be done, even upon that money. It is quite likely that someone who had strength, wisdom, and vitality, who did not live that life in those tiny, crowded rooms, in that lack of light and air, who was not bowed down with worry, but was herself economically independent of the man who earned the money, could lay out his few shillings with a better eye to scientific food value. It is quite as likely, however, that the man who earned the money would entirely refuse the scientific food, and demand his old tasty kippers and meat. It is he who has to be satisfied in the long-run, and if he desires pickles, pickles there will be. The fact that there is not enough money to buy good, healthy house-room means that appetites are jaded, and that food which would be nutritious and valuable, and would be greedily eaten by people who lived in the open air, seems tasteless and sickly to those who have slept four in a bed in a room 10 feet by 12 feet.

CHAPTER X

AMOUNT SPENT A HEAD ON FOOD—PER WEEK, PER DAY

THE remarkable thing about these budgets is the small amount left for food after all other necessaries have been paid for. When it comes to a pinch, food is the elastic item. Rent is occasionally not paid at all during a crisis, but the knowledge that it is mounting up, and that eventually it must be paid keeps these steady folk from that expedient save at the very last resource. A little less food all round, though a disagreeable experience, leaves no bill in shillings and pence to be paid afterwards. Down to a certain low minimum, therefore, food may sink before leaving the rent unpaid, or before pawning begins. That low minimum differs in different families. It is a question of the standard to which each has been accustomed, but that it is possible to be accustomed to an extraordinarily low standard these budgets amply prove.

The following are a number of weekly budgets taken at random:

Mr. A., whose house was visited from January,

1911, to February, 1912, was a railway-carriage washer, and was paid 18s. for a six days' week, alternately with 21s. for a seven days' week. His wife was a good manager, but was in delicate health. He was an extraordinarily good husband, and brought home to her his entire wage. There were three children born, and three alive.

A 21/0 *Week.*			*Left for Food*, 8/1.		
	s.	d.		s.	d.
Rent	7	0	11 loaves	2	7
Clothing club (for			1 quartern flour	0	5½
two weeks) ..	1	2	Meat	1	10
Burial insurance (for			Potatoes and greens	0	9½
two weeks) ..	1	6	½ lb. butter ..	0	6
Coal and wood ..	1	7	1 lb. jam	0	3
Coke	0	3	6 ozs. tea	0	6
Gas	0	10	2 lb. sugar ..	0	4
Soap, soda ..	0	5	1 tin of milk ..	0	4
Matches	0	1	Cocoa	0	4
Blacklead, blacking	0	1	Suet	0	2
	12	11		8	1

Average per head for food all round the family, 1s. 7½d. a week, or less than 3d. a day. But a working man cannot do on less than 6d. a day, or 3s. 6d. a week. This reduces the mother and children to 1s. 1¾d. a week, or less than 2d. a day.

Mr. B., whose house was visited from July, 1911, till September, 1912, was a printer's labourer, whose wages ranged between 20s. and 26s. a week. He usually allowed 20s. for household. There were six children born, and six alive.

November 23, 1911.			Left for Food, 7/0½.		
	s.	d.		s.	d.
Rent	8	0	14 loaves	3	2½
Burial insurance	1	8	Meat	0	10
Boot club ..	1	0	Suet	0	2
Coal	1	0	Dripping	0	6
Gas	0	8	3 ozs. tea	0	3
Wood	0	3	2 lb. sugar ..	0	4
Soap, soda ..	0	4½	2 tins of milk ..	0	6
			1 quartern flour	0	5
	12	11½	Potatoes ..	0	6
			Greens	0	4
				7	0½

Average per head for food all round the family, 10½d. a week, or 1½d. a day.

About December, 1911, the household allowance was raised to 21s. 9d., with occasional grants of 1s. towards clothes.

Mr. C., whose house was visited from November, 1910, to July, 1911, worked in a pottery. His wages were 22s. He allowed 20s. There were four children born, and four alive.

February 15, 1911.			Left for Food, 9/9½.		
	s.	d.		s.	d.
Rent	6	0	14 loaves	2	11
Burial insurance..	1	2	Meat	2	9
Coal	1	3	3 lb. sugar ..	0	6
Gas	1	2	8 ozs. tea	0	8
Soap, soda, etc. ..	0	5½	Butter	0	10
Wood	0	2	17 lbs. potatoes ..	0	10½
			1 tin of milk ..	0	3
	10	2½	Pot herbs and		
			greens ..	0	4
			1 lb. jam	0	4
			2 haddocks ..	0	4
				9	9½

Average per head for food all round the family, 1s. 7½d. a week, or 2¾d. a day. Putting the father's 3s. 6d. on one side, the mother and children average 1s. 5d. a week, or 2½d. a day.

Mr. D., whose house was visited from June, 1910, till July, 1911, was a pottery packer, making 25s. a week. He allowed 23s. There were six children born, and six alive.

November 7, 1910.	s.	d.	*Left for Food,* 10/6½	s.	d.
Rent	7	3	14 loaves ..	2	11
Burial insurance..	1	3½	Meat ..	2	8
Boot club	0	6	20 lbs. potatoes ..	0	10
Slate club	0	7	6 ozs. tea ..	0	6
Gas	0	8	Sugar ..	0	5¼
Coal	1	5	Butter ..	0	6
Soap, soda	0	5	Jam ..	0	4
Wood	0	1	Vegetables ..	0	8
Coke	0	2	Suet and lard ..	0	2½
Lamp oil ..	0	0½	Vinegar, pepper,		
Blacking ..	0	0½	and salt ..	0	1¾
			1 tin of milk ..	0	3
	12	5½	Flour ..	0	5
			Cheese ..	0	4
			Haddock ..	0	4
				10	6½

Average per head for food all round the family, 1s. 3¾d. a week, or 2¼d. a day.

Putting the father's 3s. 6d. on one side, the mother and children average 1s. a week, or 1⁵⁄₇d. a day.

Mr. E., whose house was visited from June, 1910, to October, 1912, was a painter's labourer, who never would tell his wife what he made. She had 22s. a week in summer-time, and what he

could give her in winter; never less than 20s.
when in work. The eldest girl had just got into
a soda-water factory, and was allowing 4s. a week.
Owing to a period of almost entire unemployment
in the previous winter £3 4s. was still owing for
rent when the visits began. There were seven
children alive, three dead. One son had left
home.

December 7, 1910.	s.	d.	*Left for Food*, 11/6.	s.	d.
Rent (of which 2s. is back payment)	10	0	20 loaves	4	2
Boot club ..	0	6	Meat	2	10½
Burial insurance..	0	7	2 tins of milk ..	0	6
Mangling	0	2	Sugar	0	4
Coal	1	4	Margarine ..	1	0
Gas	0	9	Potatoes	0	9
Wood	0	1	Tea	0	8
Soap, soda ..	0	4	Fish	0	4½
Linseed meal ..	0	1	Vegetables ..	0	6
Pinafore and bon-			Pepper, salt ..	0	1
net ..	0	8	Jam	0	3
	14	6		11	6

Average per head for food all round the family,
1s. 3¾d. a week, or 2¼d. a day. Putting the father's
3s. 6d. on one side, the mother and children average
1s. 1¾d. a week, or nearly 2d. a day.

To take now groups of men in the same trade
without giving the budget of each in detail will
give a more general idea. Eight carmen form
the first group. Their wages are extraordinarily
dissimilar. They, at the time their budgets passed
into the hands of the investigation, were working
for private firms, for L.C.C. contractors, and Post-

Office contractors on every kind of terms. Paid by the day or by the week, they were on night work or day work, driving one horse or two, continuously at work, or with long stretches of waiting in a yard with no shelter. One Postal van driver, who was a night worker, drove all Derby Day in between two of his nights, and got 1s. 6d. overtime for it. The case of the carman in a big West End private firm who got two days a week has been already mentioned.

The cases are as follows:

1. Wage, 26s. Allowance, 23s. 6d. 6 children; none dead.

   Rent, 5s. 6d.—2 tiny rooms. Clothing as wanted. No burial insurance.

   Average left for food on 6 weeks' full pay—14s. 5d., or 1s. 9½d. per head a week, 3d. a day: man, 3s. 6d.; mother and children, 1s. 6¾d. a week, or 2¾d. a day.

   The week that 4s. had to be spent on new boots these figures became for mother and children 11¾d. a week, or 1¾d. a day.

2. Wage, 25s. Allowance, 21s.; girl's wage, 4s.; total, 25s. 7 children alive, 1 dead, 1 away.

   Rent, 7s.—2 rooms. Clothing as wanted No burial insurance.

   Average left for food, 12s. 4½d., or 1s. 6½d. per head a week: man, 3s. 6d.; mother and children, 1s. 3¼d. a week, or 2⁵⁄₇d. a day.

3. Wage, 24s.   Allowance, 22s.   3 children alive, 1 dead.

Rent for 3 rooms, 7s.   Clothing, 6d.   Burial insurance, 8d.

Left for food, 9s. 4d., or 1s. 10½d. per head a week, 3¼d. a day: man, 3s. 6d. a week; mother and children, 1s. 5½d. a week, or 2½d. a day.

4. Wage, 24s. 9d.   Allowance, 24s.   4 children alive, 1 dead.

Rent, 8s.   Clothing, 2s. 2d.   Burial insurance, 10d.

Average left for food, 10s. 2¾d., or 1s. 8½d. per head a week, or almost 3d. a day: man, 3s. 6d.; mother and children nearly 1s. 4d. a week, or 2¼d. a day.

5. Wage, 20s.   Allowance, 19s.   4 children; none dead.

Rent, 4s. 6d. for one room.   No regular clothing. Burial insurance, 3½d.

Average left for food, 9s. 11¼d., or 1s. 7¾d. per head a week, less than 3d. a day: man, 3s. 6d.; mother and children, nearly 1s. 4d. a week, or 2¼d. a day.

6. Wage, 20s.   Allowance, 18s.   4 children alive; 5 dead.

Rent (2 rooms), 4s. 6d.   Clothing, 1s. 6d.   Burial insurance, 8½d.

Average left for food—8s. 9d., or 1s. 5½d. per head a week, 2½d. a day: man, 3s. 6d.; mother and children, 1s. 0⅗d. per head a week, less than 2d. a day.

Two cases where the weekly wage was less than 18s., owing to the men taking temporary work in unemployment:

7. Wage, 15s. Allowance, 12s. 6d. 2 children alive, 2 dead.

   Rent, 3s. 9d. (1 room). No regular clothing. No burial insurance. Has since insured.

   Average left for food—4s. 9d., or 1s. 2½d. per head a week, 2d. a day: man could not have his 3s. 6d. a week here, as that would leave only 1s. 3d. a week between mother and children. He probably manages on 2s., leaving 2s. 9d. for mother and two children.

8. Wage, 10s. Allowance, 8s. 6d. 1 child.

   Rent, 3s. 6d. (1 room). No regular clothing. No burial insurance. Has since insured.

   Average left for food—3s. 10d., or 1s. 3⅓d. per head a week, 2¼d. a day: here again the man cannot take his 3s. 6d. a week, but probably manages on about 2s., leaving 1s. 10d. a week for nursing mother.

The general average for the 8 women and 30 living children is 1s. 2⅗d. per head a week, or 2d. a day. Ten children have died, and 1 has left home, making the total of children born 41.

Another group is 3 printers' labourers, where the average for 3 women and 18 living children is 10¼d. a week, or 1½d. a day. Only 2 children have died in this group, making the total 20.

The average for the families of 2 horse-keepers is 1s. 4d. per week, or 2¼d. a day. There are 9 children living, 2 have died.

Three plumbers' and painters' labourers form another group, where 3 women and 15 living children average 1s. 1½d. a week, or almost 2d. a day. In this group 7 children have died, making a total of 22.

In the families of 2 potters' labourers, out of 10 children none have died. The 2 women and 10 children average 1s. 1½d per week, or nearly 2d. a day.

Two theatre hands out of 14 children have lost 6, and the 2 women and 8 living children average 1s. 3½d. a week, or 2¼d. a day.

The average for all the women and children within the investigation is 1s. 5½d. per head a week, or 2½d. per head a day.

This average is worked out under the supposition that the man has a uniform expenditure on his food of 3s. 6d. a week, or 6d. a day, except in about six cases, where the total amount left for food was so small that it was obvious that the man had to share more or less with the others, or they could not have lived at all. An average of six weeks was taken in each case, as the amount spent on food varied very much from week to week in some families. When clothes or sickness made an inroad on the budget down went the food.

Here is a case in point:

Mr. M.: Wage, 25s.   Allowed 23s.   Three children.

April 29, 1910.			*May* 5, 1910.		
	s.	d.		s.	d.
Rent	6	6	Rent	6	6
Coal	0	9	Coal	0	9
Wood and oil ..	0	6½	Doctor	1	0
Club	0	3	Nurse	5	0
Soap, soda ..	0	4½	Club	0	3
Boy's knickers ..	0	8¾	Burial insurance..	0	10
Burial insurance..	0	10	Soap, soda ..	0	4½
	9	11¾		14	8½

Left for food, 13/0¼, which means 9/6¼ between the mother and children, or 2/4½ per week, or 4*d.* a day.

Left for food, 8/3½, which means 4/9½ between the mother and children, or 1/2¼ per week, or 2d. a day.

Another way than that of reducing the food of hungry children is to pawn clothing when some expense must be met.

Mr. R.: Wage, 25s.; allows 21s.; six children. Daughter (partially fed at service): Wage, 4s.; allows 4s.   Total income, 29s.   Total allowance, 25s.

The daughter was told by her mistress where she was in daily service that she must come in better boots.   The average amount left for food was 11s. 3d. for the whole family of man, wife, and the five children fed at home, which means 1s. 7½d. per head a week all round the family.   Taking the usual 3s. 6d. for the man's food, there is left 7s. 9d. for the mother and children, which means 1s. 3½d. each per week, or 2¼d. per day.   The food allowance being already as low as seemed safe to go, rent being payable to a personal friend who was in difficulties herself, the pawnshop was chosen as the way out.

The statement of income given above was altered as follows:

	s.	d.
Mr. R.	21	0
S.	4	0
Made a parcel own boots	2	0
Tommy's boots	2	6
	29	6

While expenses other than food ran:

	s.	d.
Rent	7	0
Gas	1	6
Coal	2	1½
Soap, soda	0	2
Boots for S.	6	6
	17	3½

Which leaves for food all round the family, 12s. 2¼d., or an average of nearly 1s. 9d. per head a week. The average for mother and children is almost 1s. 5½d., or 2½d. a day. The sum of 4s. 6d. which was received for the boots appears later as " 4s. 8d. for boots out of pawn " in the expenditure of maternity benefit.

The sum of 3s. 6d. which is deducted for the bread-winner's food before calculating the average for mother and children is in many instances well below the actual sum spent on the man's food. This amount has been chosen as the very least the women feel themselves justified in spending.

The cases where men take 3s. or 3s. 3d. for weekday dinners are those in point. The sum of 4s. 6d. or 5s. would be nearer the mark by the end of the week, when the man has had his share of the Sunday joint, and his share, with or without " relishes," of the teas and breakfasts. In no single instance did the man seem to be having more than enough or even enough. It was evident, however, that in order to keep one person almost sufficiently fed all the rest in nearly every case had to live permanently on less than 3d. a day.

It must be remembered by those who are convinced that the working man can live well and easily on 3d. a day, because middle-class people have tried the experiment and found it possible, that the well-to-do man who may spend no more than 1s. 9d. a week on food for a month or more has not also all his other expenses cut down to their very lowest limit. The well-to-do man sleeps in a quiet, airy room, with sufficient and sanitary bedding. He has every facility for luxurious bathing and personal cleanliness. He has light and hygienic clothing; he has warmth in the winter and change of air in the summer. He can rest when he is in; he has good cooking at his command, with a sufficiency of storage, utensils, and fuel. Above all he can always stop living on 3d. a day if it does not suit him, or if his family get anxious. When his daughter needs a pair of 6s. 6d. boots he does not have to arrange an overdraft with his banker in order to meet the crisis, as the poor man does with his pawnbroker. He does not feel that all his family, well or ill, warm or cold, overworked or not, are also bound to live on 3d. a day, and are only too thankful if it does not drop to 2½d. or 2d., or even less, should under-employment or no employment come his way. It is impossible to compare the living on 3d. a day of a person all of whose other requirements are amply and sufficiently satisfied, with the living of people whose every need is thwarted and starved. Food is only half the problem. Air, light, warmth, freedom from damp, sufficient space—these, for adults—go to make up the other half, and these for young children are even of greater importance than sufficient diet.

In the households of well-to-do people two kinds of diet can be used—one for adults, the other for children. In the household which spends 10s. or even less on food, only one kind of diet is possible, and that is the man's diet. The children have what is left over. There must be a Sunday joint, or, if that be not possible, at least a Sunday dish of meat, in order to satisfy the father's desire for the kind of food he relishes, and most naturally therefore intends to have. With that will go potatoes and greens. The children share the meat, if old enough, or have potatoes and gravy. For those children too young for cold meat there may be suet pudding; but probably there is only bread and dripping, and so on and so on, not only through the week, but through the months and years. Nursery food is unknown for the children of the poor, who get only the remains of adult food.

It was reckoned by a young mother of the writer's acquaintance that the cost of *special* food used for two children in her nursery was 10s. a week—mostly spent on milk, cream, and fruit, items of diet hardly ever seen by children of the poor.

That the diet of the poorer London children is insufficient, unscientific, and utterly unsatisfactory is horribly true. But that the real cause of this state of things is the ignorance and indifference of their mothers is untrue. What person or body of people, however educated and expert, could maintain a working man in physical efficiency and rear healthy children on the amount of money which is all these same mothers have to deal with ? It would be an impossible problem if set to trained and expert people. How much more an impossible problem when set to the saddened, weakened, overburdened wives of London labourers ?

CHAPTER XI

THE POOR AND MARRIAGE

So many strictures are made on the improvident marriages of the poor that it is necessary to look at the matter from the point of view of the poor themselves.

If the poor were not improvident, they would hardly dare to live their lives at all. There is no security for them. Any work which they do may stop at a week's notice. Much work may be, and is, stopped with no notice of any kind. The man is paid daily, and one evening he is paid as usual, but told that he will not be needed again. Such a system breeds improvidence; and if casual labour and daily paid labour are necessary to society, then society must excuse the faults which are the obvious outcome of such a system.

In the case of marriage, as things now are, the moment a man's money approaches a figure which seems to him a possible one he marries. For the first year or even two years he may have less ready money but more comfort. The wife keeps their one room clean and pleasant, and cooks, none too well perhaps, but possibly with more attention to his special needs than his

former landlady did, or than his mother did, who
had her own husband as well as her other children
to cater for.   The wage may be £1 a week.   He
gives the wife 18s. and retains 2s. for himself.
The result of her management may closely
approach the following budget of two actual
young people who came within the investigation.

Mr. W., aged twenty, a toy-packer in City
warehouse—wages 20s.; allows 18s..   He has
been married eighteen months, and when this
budget was drawn up a baby was expected any
day.   His wages were raised from 18s. a year
ago.   His wife before marriage was a machinist
on piece-work, and could earn 10s. a week.   She
worked for six months after marriage, and paid
for most of the furniture in their one room; also
she provided the coming baby's clothes.   She is
clean and thrifty, writes a good hand, and keeps
excellent accounts.   She is nineteen.

Out of the 2s. retained by the husband, he pays
6d. a week into a clothing club, and of course his
4d. is deducted for State Insurance.   With the rest
" he does what he likes."   Sometimes he likes to
give the wife an extra penny for her housekeeping.
The menu, from the list of food purchases given
on next page, appears to consist of a sufficiency
of bread, of meat, of potatoes, and perhaps of
greens, as the husband's dinners eaten away from
home probably include greens for him.   Some
cold meat, with bread and butter and tea, would

be provided for the evening meal; bread, butter, and tea would be the invariable breakfast.

Date of budget, January 16, 1913:

	s.	d.
Rent (one good room upstairs; two windows) ..	5	0
Burial insurance	0	3
Boot club	0	6
Coal (1 cwt. stove coal for foreign stove, which stands out into the room, and will be very dangerous when the baby begins to crawl) ..	1	3
Gas	0	8
Soap	0	3
Oil	0	2
Matches	0	1½
	8	2½

Left for food   ..   9s. 9½d.

	s.	d.
Six loaves	1	4½
Husband's dinners (he is given 6d. daily by his wife for his dinner, which he eats away from home)	3	0
Meat	3	2½
½ lb. butter	0	6
1 lb. flour	0	1½
1 tin of milk	0	4
4 ozs. tea	0	4
1 lb. moist sugar	0	2
½ lb. dripping	0	3
8 lbs. potatoes	0	4
4 lbs. greens	0	2
	9	9½

An average per head of 4s. 10¾d. a week for food

If the wages never rise, and if the family grows larger, the amounts spent on burial insurance, soap, coal, gas, and, later on, rent will increase, leaving less and less for food, with more people to feed on the less amount. Extra bedding will eventually have to be bought, though the parents will naturally put off that moment as long as possible. Should the wage rise gradually to 24s., or even 25s., it would not all go upon the general living. The man would naturally take a larger amount of pocket-money, and out of the extra sum which he might allow the wife, he would certainly expect better living. A " relish to his tea," costing 2d. a day, mounts up to 1s. a week, and a " rasher to his breakfast " costs the same. So an increase of 2s. might be completely swallowed up in extra food for the worker. And it would be really needed by him, as his proportion of the money spent would tend to diminish with more mouths to fill.

Another instance of a young couple starting on £1 a week is that of Mr. H., who is twenty-two, and works in a brewery. Every third week he has night work. He allows his wife his whole wage. There is one child of six months. The wife is twenty. She worked in a polish factory until marriage, when she was dismissed, with a small bonus, as the firm does not employ married women. With the bonus she helped to furnish. She is an excellent housewife, and keeps her room comfortable.

Date of budget, January 16, 1913 (see p. 150).

Owing to Mr. H. getting home to his meals, there is more elasticity in this menu. Much less meat is eaten, and fish and bacon appear instead. More bread, more tea, more vegetables are eaten,

	s.	d.
Rent (one room, small; one window, upstairs)	3	6
Husband's fares	1	0
Husband's pocket-money	1	0
State sickness insurance	0	4
Four weeks' burial insurance (Mr. H. had been ill on half pay, and burial insurance had stood over)	1	0
Soap, soda	0	3½
1 cwt. coal	1	6
Gas	0	6
Wood	0	2
Newspaper	0	1
Boracic powder	0	1
Cotton	0	2
Needles	0	0½
Buttons	0	1
Paid off loan (5s. borrowed from a brother during husband's illness)	1	0
	10	9

This leaves for food, 9s. 3d. between three people, or an average of 3s. 1d. a head.

	s.	d.
9 loaves	1	10½
8 ozs. tea	0	8
2 lbs. moist sugar	0	4
1 tin of milk (a smaller tin than Mrs. W.'s)	0	3½
½ lb. butter (slightly better than Mrs. W.'s)	0	7
2 lbs. flour	0	3
8 lbs. potatoes	0	4
Vegetables	0	7
Salt, mustard, sauce	0	2½
Fruit	0	6
Fish	1	0
Bacon	0	4½
Mineral water (recommended by doctor for Mr. H. during his illness)	0	3
Meat	2	0
	9	3

and fruit is added.   The usual breakfast is bread,
butter, and tea; the dinner a small amount of
meat, with potatoes and vegetables; the evening
meal, fish or bacon, with potatoes, as well as the
eternal bread, butter, and tea.   All these four
young people are steady and intelligent.   They
have enough to eat, but they are put to it for
proper clothing already.   The H.'s will have to
move sooner than the W.'s if their family increases,
as their room, though a pleasant one, is not above
half the size of the other.

It is obvious that with both these young men
marriage is, so far, both pleasant and successful.
It is worth the sacrifice in pocket-money which
it must entail upon them.   Their working life is
much the same as it was during their bachelor-
hood, while their free time is more comfortable
and more interesting.   Should they have waited
to marry until later in life, they would probably
have lived no cheaper as bachelors, though the
money would have been spent differently, and they
would have been less wholesomely comfortable.

The young women's lives are far more changed.
They tell you that, though they are a bit lonely
at times, and miss the companionship of the
factory life and the money of their own to spend,
and are rather frightened at the swift approach
of motherhood, " You get accustomed to it," and
" It won't be so lonely when the baby comes,"
and " He's very handy when he's at home."   The
first baby is a source of great interest and pleasure

to both parents, especially if it is well managed and does not cry at night, though one young father who was accustomed to a restless baby said he " missed it ter'ble at night " when it was away in hospital. It is different when the children multiply and the room becomes crowded and food is less plentiful.   Then the case of the man is hard and unattractive; the amount of self-sacrifice demanded of him, if he be at all tender-hearted towards his family, is outrageous. He must never smoke, he must never take a glass of ale ; he must walk to and from his work in all weathers; he must have no recreations but the continual mending of his children's boots.; he must neither read nor go to picture palaces nor take holidays, if he is to do all that social reformers expect of him when they theoretically parcel out his tiny income. Needless to say, the poorly paid man is not so immeasurably superior to the middle-class man in the matter of self-denial and self-control as he seems expected to be.   He does smoke, he does sometimes take a glass of ale; he does, in fact, appropriate a proportion of the money he earns to his own pleasure.   It is not a large proportion as a rule, but it upsets the nice calculations which are based upon the supposition that a man earning 25s. a week spends every penny of it in the support of his family.   He is, most probably, a hard-working, steady, sober man; but he may spend perhaps 2d. a day on beer, 1d. a day on tobacco, and 2d. a day on tram fares, and that without being a monster of selfishness, or wishing to deprive his children of their food.   In most budgets he keeps from 2s. to 2s. 6d. for himself, in some 5s. or 6s., and in some nothing.   He varies as his brethren vary in other classes.   Sometimes he walks to and from work; sometimes he pays his fares out of the money he keeps; and sometimes he gets them paid out of the money with which he supplies his wife.

Though fond of the children when they are there, this life of stress and strain makes the women dread nothing so much as the conviction that there is to be still another baby with its inevitable consequences—more crowding, more illness, more worry, more work, and less food, less strength, less time to manage with.

There are people who argue that marriage should be put off by the poor until they have saved up enough to secure their economic independence, and that it would not hurt young men on £1 a week to put off marriage till they are thirty, they, meantime, saving hard during those ten years.   Should the poorly paid workman overcome his young impulse to marry the moment his wage reaches £1 a week, and should he remain a bachelor until thirty, it is quite certain that he would not marry at all.   This may be a good thing or a bad thing, but it would be so.   A man who for ten years had had the spending of 20s. a week—and it is a sum which is soon spent without providing luxuries—would not, at thirty, when perhaps cold reason would direct his impulse, feel inclined to share his £1 a week with an uncertain number of other people. His present bent is towards married life. It provides him for the first year or two with attention to his comfort and with privacy and freedom for his personality, as well as satisfying his natural craving for sex-relationship. Should he thwart that impulse, he, being an average, normal man, will have to find other ways of dealing with these desires of his. He is not likely to starve every instinct for ten years in order, perhaps, to save a sum which might bring in an income of a couple of shillings a week to add to his weekly wage. He would know, by the time he was thirty, that even 22s. a week does not guarantee a family against misery and want. The self-sacrifice demanded of the father of even a small family on such an income would appal him.

The young couple who marry and live contentedly on 20s. a week are usually members of families of at least four or five persons, and have struggled through their childhood on their share of an income which may have been anything from 20s. to 25s. or 26s. a week. Their standard of comfort is disastrously low, and they do not for the first year or two realise that even two or three children will develop into a burden which is too great for their strength. It is not the greater number of children alone: it is the greater cost of accommodating, feeding, and clothing boys and girls as they get older which increases the strain. Moreover, the separation of interests soon begins to show itself. The husband goes to the same work—hard, long, and monotonous—but at least a change from the growing discomfort of the home. He gets accustomed to seeing his wife slave, and she gets accustomed to seeing him appear and disappear on his daily round of work, which gradually appeals less and less to her imagination, till, at thirty, she hardly knows what his duties are— so overwhelmed is she in the flood of her own most absorbing duties and economies. Her economies interfere with his comfort, and are irksome to him; so he gets out of touch with her point of view. He cannot see why the cooking should be less satisfactory than it used to be, and says so. She knows she needs a new saucepan, but cannot possibly afford to buy one, and says so. He makes his wife the same allowance, and expects the same amount of food. She has more mouths to fill, and grows impatient because he does not understand that, though their first baby did not seem to make much difference, a boy of three, plus a baby, makes the old problem into quite a new one.

One of her questions is the balance between rent and food, which is of enormous importance. Yet she never can feel certain that she has found the right solution. Shall they all live in one room ? Or shall they take two basement rooms at an equally low rent, but spend more on gas

and coal, and suffer more from damp and cold ?
Or shall they take two rooms above stairs and take
the extra rent out of the food ?   Her own appetite may not be very large, so she decides perhaps
on the two better rooms upstairs. She may
decide wisely, as we think, but the sacrifice in food
is not to be ignored in its results on the health of
the children.

Another of her problems is, How is she to keep
her husband, the bread-winner, in full efficiency
out of the few shillings she can spend on food, and
at the same time satisfy the appetites of the
children ?   She decides to feed him sufficiently
and to make what is over do for herself and the
children.   This is not considered and thought-out
self-sacrifice on her part.   It is the pressure of
circumstances.   The wage-earner must be fed.
The arrangement made between husband and
wife in cases where the man's work is at a distance—that 6d. a day, or 3s. a week, should be
allowed by her for his dinners—may have begun,
as in the case already quoted, before any children
had appeared, and may continue when there are
six children. Even if the wage has increased,
and if, instead of 20s., the worker is getting 23s.
or 24s., he probably keeps an extra shilling for
himself.   Instead of allowing his wife 18s. a
week, he allows her 20s. or 21s.   If she has
several children, the father's weekly 3s. for dinner
is far harder to compass than when she managed
for two only on 18s.   Rent, instead of being

from 3s. 6d. to 5s. for one " good " upstairs room, amounts to from 6s. to 7s. for two upstairs rooms, or, if house-room be sacrificed to food, rent may be 5s. 6d. for two deadly basement rooms. Insurance has mounted from 3d. a week to 9d. a week.   Gas which was 6d. is now 1s., on account of the extra cooking.   Soap and other cleaning materials have increased in quantity, and therefore in expense from 2d. to 5½d.   Clothing is a problem for which very few weekly figures are available.   It must be covered by payments to clothing and boot clubs, or each article must be bought when needed.   In any case the expense is greater and the amount of money available for food grows less.   The unvarying amount paid for the bread-winner's necessary daily food becomes a greater proportion of the food bill, and leaves all the increasing deficit to be met out of the food of the mother and children.   It is unavoidable that it should be so; nobody wastes time thinking about it; but the fact that it is so forces the mother to take a different point of view from that of the father.   So each of them gradually grows to understand the other less.

Both parents are probably devoted to the children.   The husband, who is sick of his wife's complaints, and can't be bothered with her story of how she has no boots to wear, listens with sympathy and understanding to her tale of woe about Tommy having no boots to his feet.   The boy who cannot speak at three years of age, or the girl who is deficient in weight, in height, and in wits, often is the father's special pet, for whom he will sacrifice both food and sleep, while the mother's whole life is spent in a dreary effort to do her best for them all round.

Much has been said and written, and much more will be said and written, on the question of the poor and large families. We wrangle as to whether their numerous children are an improvidence and an insult to the community, or whether, on the contrary, the poorest class is the only class which, in that respect, does its duty to the nation. One thing is quite certain, and it is that it would be as unthinkable as impossible to bring compulsion to bear on the poor because they are poor. For those who deplore large families in the case of poor people, it must be a comfort to remember a fact which experience shews us, that as poverty decreases, and as the standard of comfort rises, so does the size of the family diminish. Should we be able to conquer the problem of poverty, we should automatically solve the problem of the excessively large family.

CHAPTER XII

MOTHERS' DAYS

In a previous chapter some description was given of the way in which the women arrange their work. It is the province of this chapter to describe in greater detail the "days" of several of the women—mounting up, as they do gradually from the day of the young mother of one baby to that of the worn woman of thirty-eight with eight children under thirteen. Washing-day was not considered fair by the mothers. They said, "You'd expeck ter be a bit done-like washin'-day;" so an ordinary day was chosen in every case. They anxiously explained that the time-table form in which the visitor took the day wasn't fair either because, "You jest as likely as not get a bit be'ind if 'indered." But the subject was so richly interesting, and led up to such absorbing anecdotes when left to the mothers' taste in method, that the time-table form had to be used in self-protection by the visitor. The following is a specimen of a mother's way of telling it: "Me young man 'as ter be up abart five. E's a fair whale at sleep. If I didn't wake 'im 'e'd be late all the days in the year: I tell yer. E' come 'ome

abart six, 'n soon's 'e's 'ad 'is tea 'e's that sleepy
agen you'd 'ardly get a word off 'im.''   Gently
reminded here that it is her own day that is
required, she continues: '' Oh, me ?   Well, I tells
yer I wakes 'im at five.   I 'as ter give 'im a good
thump, an' 'e gets up quiet-like if 'e can; but 'e
generly can't, an' then the kids begin talkin', an'
I 'as a fair job ter keep 'em in bed.   See that one
with red 'air—'e's a fair treat in the mornin's,'' etc.

The first day given is that of a young mother
aged twenty, with her first baby—a fat, round
morsel who may be called well cared for after
the initial disadvantage of living with its parents
in one small and dismal room has been recognised.   The young mother owns a large sewing-
machine, of which she is intolerably proud.   As
Lambeth mothers' days go, hers is a very easy
one.

6.0.—Get up and light fire.

6.15.—Wake husband, who has to be off by
seven; get his breakfast.

6.30.—Give him his breakfast, and while he
eats it, nurse baby.

7.0.—When he has gone, put baby down and
eat breakfast.

7.30.—Wash up; do a little washing every day
for baby; air bed; carry down dirty water; bring
fresh up from yard (second floor).

8.30.—Baby wakes; give her a bath and dress
her; nurse her; let her lie and kick while sweeping
room and blacking grate and scrubbing stairs;

make bed; carry baby out, and do shopping for dinner.

11.0.—Come in and nurse baby; get dinner ready.

12.15.—Husband comes in; give him dinner. He leaves a few minutes to one o'clock.

1.0.—Wash up, and nurse baby; take her out for a walk, if fine, for as long as can bear it. She is heavy. Come in when time to nurse her again, and sit down to sew. Make all her clothes and most of own, and mend husband's.

4.30.—Get tea ready and cook relish.

5.0.—Husband comes in; give him tea, and help him clean himself in warm water; wash up and carry down dirty water, and bring up clean water.

6.0.—Nurse baby and get her to bed; husband not strong, and likes to go to bed early; sit and sew till time to nurse baby at nine o'clock. Get everything ready for morning.

9.30.—Go to bed.

One week in every three the husband works at night, instead of the day. The wife finds this less convenient for her, and is certain that it over-strains him, as he cannot sleep properly in the day, though she tries to be as quiet as ever she can. But the baby is bound to disturb him, as the room is very small. During this week, dinner is whenever he gets up, and all the cleaning and washing has to be squeezed in afterwards.

The next case is that of Mrs. O., who has but two children alive, both very young. Two rooms have to be looked after, and extremely well looked after, for Mr. O. is the gentleman who keeps 5s. a week out of 25s., and expects 4s. 4d. a week spent on his own extra food. He likes the place nice, and cannot see that his wife need ever go out except for the purpose of buying the family food. He believes that women are prone to extravagance in dress, and does not encourage Mrs. O. in any such nonsense. When it was necessary that she should come once a fortnight to the weighing centre, to have the baby weighed, the price of a pair of boots had to be saved out of several weeks' food, much to the annoyance of Mr. O., who could not understand why any of his family should ever leave the two rooms where they live.

Her day runs as follows:

7.0.—Get up and get husband's breakfast; nurse baby while he has it.

7.30.—He goes to work. Get little girl dressed, get her breakfast, and have it with her.

8.0.—Wash up.

8.30.—Get baby's bath and wash and dress him.

9.0.—Nurse him and put him to sleep.

9.30.—Do beds and sweep bedroom, and carry up water (first floor).

11.0.—Start to make little girl a frock till baby wakes; nurse him when he does.

12.15.—Get dinner for self and child ready (husband has dinner away from home).

1.0.—Have dinner.

1.30.—Nurse baby and clear away and wash up dinner things. Sweep and scrub floor and passage, clean grate; every other week do stairs.

2.30.—Wash myself and little girl, and take children out till four.

4.0.—Get tea and nurse baby.

4.30.—Clear away, and get husband's tea; wait for him till he comes in; very uncertain, between five and seven o'clock; go on making frock till he does.

6.0.—Put children to bed.

6.30.—Wash up husband's tea things, if he has finished. As soon as he has finished, he changes and goes out.

8.0.—Go up The Walk for shopping for next day, leaving children in bed.

9.0.—Mend husband's clothes, and go on with frock till ten.

10.0.—Nurse baby and make both children comfortable for the night.

11.0.—If husband has come in, go to bed.

This is not a hard day as things go in Lambeth. The noticeable thing about it is its loneliness. Mrs. O. knows nothing of her neighbours, and, until the visitor insisted on the children's getting out every afternoon, and agitated for the boots, Mrs. O. never took them out. She did her shopping at night in order that her old slippers might not be seen. She sat indoors and mended and made clothes in her neat room, while her pale little girl amused herself as best she could and the baby lay on the bed. The husband merely ate and slept at home. He was a particularly respectable and steady man, who kept his clothes neat and his person scrupulously clean. His wife ministered to him in every way she could, but saw nothing of him. He took no interest in the little daughter, but was proud of the boy, and it was by means of the boy's need of fresh air that he was persuaded to allow his wife to save for her boots. For her he did not consider them necessary, as he was in favour of women staying at home and minding the house.

The next day is that of a woman who lives in one room in buildings, with her husband and four children. She is rather self-assertive and talkative, very clean, rougher in her manner of speaking to her children than most of the mothers, but very affectionate to both children and husband. Her old mother, whom she partially feeds, is a great deal with her, and helps in the household work. Her day is rather an easy one for Lambeth. The eldest child is eight years old, and the baby is a few months. As the room is in " buildings," she has water on the same level, so has not to carry it up or down stairs.

4.30.—Wake husband, who has to be at work about five o'clock. He is carman for an L.C.C. contractor. Get him off if possible without waking the four children. He has a cup of tea before going, but breakfasts away from home. If baby wakes, nurse him.

7.0.—Nurse baby.

7.15.—Get up and light fire, wake children, wash two eldest ones. Get breakfast for self and children.

8.0.—Breakfast.

8.30.—Tidy two children for school and start them off at 8.45.

9.0.—Clear away and wash up; wash and dress boy of three; bathe and dress baby.

10.0.—Nurse baby and put him to bed.

10.30.—Turn down beds, clean grate, scrub floor.

11.30.—Make beds.

12.0.—Mother, who has done the marketing, brings in the food; begin to cook dinner.

12.15.—Children all in, lay dinner, and, with mother's help, tidy children for it.

1.0.—Dinner, which mother serves while Mrs. G. nurses baby who wakes about then.

1.30.—Tidy children for school again.

1.45.—Start them off and sit down with mother to their own dinner; wash up, tidy room, clean themselves.

3.0.—Go out, if it is not washing-day or day for doing the stairs, with baby and boy of three.

3.45.—Come in and get tea for children. Put boy of three to sleep, nurse baby.

4.15.—Children come in.

4.30.—Give children tea.

5.0.—Wash up and tidy room. Tidy children and self.

6.0.—Take up boy of three and go out for a " blow in the street " with all four children.

7.0.—Come in and put children to bed. Nurse baby.

7.30.—Husband returns; get his supper.

8.0.—Sit down and have supper with him.

8.30.—Clear away and wash up. Sew while husband goes to bed. " Talk wile 'e's doin' it."

9.0.—Send mother off. Get everything ready for the morning. Mend husband's clothes as soon as he gets them off.

10.0.—Nurse baby and go to bed.

We now come to the day of a mother of six children, with two rooms to keep. Mrs. T., whose menu has already been given, is the wife of a builder's handy-man on 25s. a week. The two rooms are upstairs in a small house, and, as there is no water above the ground floor, Mrs. T. has a good deal of carrying of heavy pails of water both upstairs and down. She is gentle and big and slow, never lifts her voice or gets angry, but seems always tired and dragged. She is very clean and orderly. Her husband is away all day; but he dislikes the noise of a family meal, and insists on having both breakfast and tea cooked specially for himself, and eats alone.

6.0.—Nurses baby.

6.30.—Gets up, calls five children, puts kettle on, washes " necks " and " backs " of all the children, dresses the little ones, does hair of three girls.

7.30.—Gets husband's breakfast, cooks bloater, and makes tea.

8.0.—Gives him breakfast alone, nurses baby while he has it, and cuts slices of bread and dripping for children.

8.30.—He goes, gives children breakfast, sends them off to school at 8.50, and has her own.

9.0.—Clears away and washes up breakfast things.

9.30.—Carries down slops, and carries up water from the yard; makes beds.

10.0.—Washes and dresses baby, nurses him, and puts him to bed.

11.0.—Sweeps out bedroom, scrubs stairs and passage.

12.0.—Goes out and buys food for the day. Children home at 12.15.

12.30.—Cooks dinner; lays it.

1.0.—Gives children dinner and nurses baby.

1.45.—Washes hands and faces, and sees children off to school.

2.0.—Washes up dinner things, scrubs out kitchen, cleans grate, empties dirty water, and fetches more clean from yard.

3.0.—Nurses baby.

3.30.—Cleans herself and begins to mend clothes.

4.15.—Children all back.

4.30.—Gives them tea.

5.0.—Clears away and washes up, nurses the baby, and mends clothes till 6.30.

6.30.—Cooks husband's tea.

7.0.—Gives husband tea alone.

7.30.—Puts younger children to bed.

8.0.—Tidies up, washes husband's tea things, sweeps kitchen, and mends clothes, nurses baby, puts elder children to bed.

8.45.—Gets husband's supper; mends clothes.

10.0.—Nurses baby, and makes him comfortable for the night.

10.30.—Goes to bed.

The last "day" is that of the woman who has eight children under thirteen. The fact that her husband works at night enables the family to sleep seven in one room—the mother and five children by night and the husband by day; in the other bedroom three older children sleep in a single bed. This woman is tall and would be good-looking if her figure were not much misshapen. She has quantities of well-washed hair, and good teeth; but her face is that of a woman of fifty. She is thirty-eight. She can stand very little advice or argument, and simply does not listen when either are offered to her. She seems always to be hearing a baby wake, or correcting a child of two, or attending to the soiled face of the little girl of three and a half, who is so much smaller than her younger brother. She once went for a fortnight's change to the seaside. The visitor asked her, when she came back, what she had most enjoyed. She thought for a considerable time, and then made the following statement: " I on'y 'ad two babies along of me, an' wen I come in me dinner was cooked for me."

There is no doubt that if Mrs. B. were stronger she would not need to nurse her baby quite so often. He is small and hungry, and will soon need to be weaned if his mother is to work as hard as she does on ordinary days; with extra exertion on washing-days, and extra noise and interruption in holiday-time.

Mr. B., printer's labourer ; wage 30s.; allows 28s. ; night worker. Eight children ; eldest, a girl of twelve years; youngest, three months.

6.45.—Nurses baby.

7.0.—Rises, calls children, lights fire and puts on kettle, washes and dresses elder four children. Girl of twelve can do for herself. Boy of ten can do all but his ears.

8.0.—Gets breakfast; bread and butter and tea for children.

8.15.—Gives children breakfast; gets them off to school by 8.45.

8.45.—Nurses baby.

9.0.—Fetches down the three babies, washes and dresses them; gives the two bigger their breakfast.

9.30.—Husband comes home; cooks him rasher or haddock.

10.0.—Gives him his breakfast, and goes upstairs to tidy her room for husband to sleep in; makes her bed for him, which has been airing since seven o'clock. Turns out and airs beds in other room, taking two elder babies with her.

10.30.—Clears away and washes up all the breakfast things.

11.0.—Nurses baby and puts all three to sleep.

11.15.—Goes out to buy dinner.

11.30.—Prepares dinner.

12.10.—Children all home again; goes on with dinner.

1.0.—Lays and serves dinner.

1.30.—Washes hands and faces of five children, and sends them off to school.

1.45.—Nurses baby, and sits down till 2.30.

2.30.—Washes up and begins cleaning. Sweeps kitchen, scullery, and passage, scrubs them, cleans grate; three babies to mind all the time.

4.10.—Children all home again; gets their tea, nurses baby.

4.30.—Clears away, and begins to cook husband's dinner.

5.0.—Husband wakes; gives him dinner; sits down while she cuts his food for him to take to work, keeping babies and children as quiet as she can.

6.0.—Nurses baby.

6.30.—He starts for work. She makes children's beds, turns out his, airs his room, and makes his bed up for herself and three children to sleep in at night. All water used in bedrooms has to be carried upstairs, and when used, carried down.

7.30.—Washes and puts to bed two babies.

8.0.—Nurses baby.

8.15.—Washes and puts to bed elder children.

8.45.—Mends clothes.

10.0.—Nurses baby and puts him to bed.

10.30.—Goes to bed; nurses baby twice in the night.

There is no room for the " day " of the mother who bakes her own bread. Her husband, who works for a Post-Office contractor, is on night-duty, and spends most of the day at home. He is an old soldier, as are an appreciable proportion of these low-wage men. He helps his wife in the housework and the cooking, and their home is one of the most spotless the visitor has seen. When his wife was sent to the seaside for two weeks, he managed entirely for himself and the five children. His " day " would have been very valuable could the visitor have persuaded him to make it out for those two weeks. He apologised to her for not making the money go as far as " mother " did, for buying loaves and not baking the bread, for scrubbing without soap, which he had forgotten to buy; but a detailed account of his day he could not give. He was a guardsman when in the army, and stands six feet in his socks. He weighs eleven stone at thirty-six—a stone less than when he was serving. Here are the accounts for his two weeks, alongside a budget of his wife's, with which to compare (see p. 173). He sent them with the following letter:

" Mrs. R.,—

" Unfortunately I had Rachel at home on the Friday as Mother went away on the Thursday. I could not do on the money ; I had as you will see to borrow 5s. as well as putting the whole of my money in the house. The last week I managed better, but had to miss my club. I should have sent the list down to you each week but Mother forgot to ask me to do so."

The reference to Rachel is that she lost her situation just as his wife left home. He had her food to get as well as the other children's during his fortnight. She is an excellent worker, and got another place as soon as her mother came back.

The items " ink, pen, nibs, stationery, and stamps " directly mother went away are rather touching. The enormous consumption of margarine—3s. 6d. as against 1s. 6d.—is an instance of the way in which the father is kept in ignorance of the privations which are undergone by his family. Directly he was left in charge, this father allowed margarine all round on the same scale as he had always used it himself, with the result of more than doubling the amount spent on it. The item in his first week of 2s. 3d. for gas when there was no baking to be done, as against his wife's 2s. when there was, shows that the $\frac{1}{2}$ cwt. of coal did not suffice him, and that he cooked by gas. The savings he made in his second week are most entertaining. No soap or cleaning material of

Mrs. H., June 18.

	s.	d.
Income:		
Mr. H.	21	0
Rachel	4	0
Bread sold	0	9
	25	9
Rent	6	6
Gas	2	0
Coal	0	8½
Soap, soda, etc.	0	7¼
Blacklead, hearthstone	0	1½
Matches	0	1½
Stockings	0	4¾
Cottons	0	3
Knickers (two boys)	1	4
Flour and yeast	5	5
Meat	2	6
Margarine	1	6
Sugar	0	7
Tea	0	6
Cocoa, coffee	1	0
Potatoes	0	7
Vegetables	0	5
Cow's milk	0	1½
Oatmeal	0	5
Salt	0	1½
	25	9

Mr. H., June 25.

	s.	d.
Income:		
Mr. H., whole wage	25	0
Borrowed	5	0
	30	0
Rent	6	6
Gas	2	3
Coal	0	8½
Soap	0	5
Blacklead, etc.	0	1½
Matches	1	6
Washing	1	2
Slate club	0	4
National insurance	1	0
Hospital	0	1
Tobacco	3	3¾
Ink, pen, nibs	2	2¼
Stationery	0	1
Stamps	0	4
Bread	5	0
Meat	3	6
Margarine	3	8
Sugar	0	6
Tea	0	6
Cocoa, coffee	1	6
Potatoes	0	0
Vegetables	0	5½
Cow's milk	0	2
Rice	0	0
Salt, pepper	0	2
	30	0

Mr. H., July 2.

	s.	d.
Income:		
Mr. H.	25	0
Rent	6	6
Gas	1	6
Coal	—	
Soap, soda	—	
Blacklead, etc.	—	
Matches	1	0
Washing	2	0
Boots (Tommy)	—	
Club	0	4
National insurance	1	0
Hospital	1	1
Tobacco	1	1½
Boot polish	0	1½
Stamps	0	3½
Tram fares	0	3
Bread	4	2
Meat	2	0
Margarine	3	0
Sugar	0	8
Tea	0	6
Cocoa, coffee	—	
Potatoes	1	0
Vegetables	—	
Cow's milk	0	5½
Oatmeal, rice	—	
	25	0

any kind, no coal, no matches; and yet the grate did not look bad nor the floor either when the visitor saw them at the end of his strenuous time. The amount spent on tobacco, his one luxury, is interesting, as it is the sole instance in which this item is accounted for in the budgets. He was obliged to put every penny of his wage into the general fund during those two weeks. The penny for the hospital is a very common payment in Lambeth—one which always comes out of the man's private purse. Incidentally, we are able to construct his own private budget of 4s. pocket-money out of this budget of his. It must run something like this:

	s.	d.
National insurance	0	4
Slate club	1	2
Hospital	0	1
Tobacco	1	6
Fares, etc.	0	11
	4	0

That the children of the poor suffer from insufficient attention and care is not because the mother is lazy and indifferent to her children's well-being. It is because she has but one pair of hands and but one overburdened brain. She can just get through her day if she does everything she has to do inefficiently. Give her six children, and between the bearing of them and the rearing of them she has little extra vitality left for scientific cooking, even if she could afford the necessary time and appliances. In fact, one woman is not equal to the bearing and efficient, proper care of six children. She can make one bed for four of them; but if she had to make four beds; if she even had to separate the boys from the girls, and keep two rooms clean instead of one; if she had to make proper clothing and keep those clothes properly washed and ironed and mended; if she had to give each child a daily bath, and had to attend thoroughly to teeth, noses, ears, and eyes; if she had to cook really nourishing food, with adequate utensils and dishes, and had to wash up these utensils and dishes after every meal—she would need not only far more money, but far more help. The children of the poor suffer from want of room, want of light, want of air, want of warmth, want of sufficient and proper food, and want of clothes, because there is not enough to pay for these necessaries. They also suffer from want of cleanliness, want of attention to health, want of peace and quiet, because the strength of their mothers is not enough to provide these necessary conditions.

CHAPTER XIII

THE CHILDREN

In this investigation forty-two families have been visited. Of these, eight, owing to various reasons, were visited but for a short time. Three were given up after several weeks, because the husbands objected to the household accounts being shown to the visitor; and here it would be interesting to mention that in three other cases, not reckoned in the investigation, the husbands refused after the first week for the same reason as soon as they thoroughly realised the scope of the inquiry. In four cases the babies were born too soon, and lived but a few hours. The investigation was primarily on infantile mortality, so that it automatically ceased with the child's death. One family moved out of London before the child's birth. There remain, therefore, thirty-four babies who were watched and studied by the visitors for many months. In every case but one these children were normal, and thriving at birth. Only one weighed less than 6 lbs.; four more weighed less than 7 lbs.; fifteen more weighed less than 8 lbs.; ten more weighed less than 9 lbs.; and four weighed over 9 lbs. The average weight at birth for the whole number was 7 lbs. 10 ozs. The child which weighed 5 lbs. 12 ozs. at birth was always sickly, and died of diarrhœa and sickness during the hot August of 1911 at the age of six months. Her mother was a delicate woman, and had come through a time of dire stress when her husband was out of work for four months before this child was born. A baby born since, which does not appear in this investigation, is now about five months old. Not one of the others seemed otherwise than sound and healthy, and able to thrive on the nourishment which was provided for their special benefit by the investigation. One child, however, a beautiful boy of five months, who weighed 7 lbs. 12 ozs. at birth, and 14 lbs. 14 ozs. at twenty weeks, died suddenly of bronchitis in December, 1910. His mother's health record was bad. He was the sixth child she had lost out of eleven. She was an extraordinarily tidy, clean woman, and an excellent manager; but her father had died of consumption, and she was one of those mothers who economised in rent in order to feed her flock more adequately. She paid 5s. a week for very dark ground-floor rooms. The death of the child was so sudden and unexpected that an inquest was held. The mother was horrified and bewildered at the entrance of police officers into her home. She wrung her hands and repeated over and over, " I done all I could !" and never shook off the impression that some disgrace attached to her. The burial insurance money paid by the company was £1. Five shillings specially earned by the mother and 5s. lent by a friend brought up the amount to the necessary 30s., and the humble funeral took place. The child was buried in a common grave with seven other coffins of all sizes.

With these two exceptions, the babies all lived to be over a year. They usually did fairly well, unless some infection from the elder children gave them a bad cold, or measles, or whooping-cough, when some of them had a hard struggle to live, and their convalescence was much retarded by the close air and overcrowding of their unhygienic surroundings. Compared with babies who were fighting such surroundings without special nourishment, they did well, but compared with the children of well-to-do people they did badly indeed !

The ex-baby, where such a person existed, was nearly always undersized, delicate, and peevish. Apart from such causes as insufficient and improper food, crowded sleeping quarters, and wretched clothing, this member of the family specially suffered from want of fresh air. Too young to go out alone, with no one to carry it now the baby had come, it lived in the kitchen, dragging at its mother's skirts, much on its legs, but never in the open air. One of the conveniences most needed by poor mothers is a perambulator which will hold, if possible, her two youngest children. With such a vehicle, there would be some sort of chance of open air and change of scene so desperately necessary for the three house-bound members of the family. As it is, the ex-baby is often imprisoned in a high chair, where it cannot fall into the fire, or pull over the water-can, or shut its finger in the crack of the door, or get at the food. But here it is deprived of exercise and freedom of limb, and develops a fretful, thwarted character, which renders it even more open to disease than the rest of the family, though they share with it all the other bad conditions.

There is no doubt that the healthy infant at birth is less healthy at three months, less healthy still at a year, and often by the time it is old enough to go to school it has developed rickets or lung trouble through entirely preventible causes.

To take several families individually, and go through their history, may serve as illustration of the way in which children who begin well are worn down by the conditions round them:

Mr. A., whose house was visited all the year of 1909, was originally a footman in one of the houses of a large public school. He seemed at the time of visiting to be fairly strong and wiry. He was about 5 feet 8 inches in height, well educated, and very steady. His wife had been a lady's-maid, who had saved a little money, which she sank in a boarding-house kept by her-self and her sister. The boarding-house did not pay, and when Mrs. A. married, the sister went back into the service of the lady with whom she had been before. Mr. A. left his position as footman, and became a bus conductor in one of the old horse-bus companies. When visited in 1909 he had been fifteen years in his position, but owing to the coming of motor traffic, his employers gradually ran fewer buses, and his work became more casual. He was paid 4s. a day, and got four days' work a week, with an occasional fifth day. He had to present himself every morning, and wait a certain time before he knew whether he would be employed or not. All that he made he brought home. His wife, who by the time the visits began was worn and delicate, was a well-educated woman, and an excellent manager. She saved on all the 20s. weeks in order to have a little extra for the 16s. weeks. Her sister in service often came to the rescue when extra trouble, such as illness or complete unemployment, visited the household. There were five children after the baby of the investigation arrived. The eldest, a girl, was consumptive; the next, a boy, was short in one leg, and wore a surgical boot; the next, a girl, was the airless ex-baby, and suffered with its eyes; and only the new-born child, weighing 9 lbs., seemed to be thriving and strong. The average per week for food was 1s. a head for man, woman, and children. Presently the conductor's work stopped altogether. No more horse-buses were run on that particular route, and motor-buses did not come that way.

Mr. A. was out of work. He used to bring in odd sums of money earned in all sorts of ways between tramping after a new job. The eldest girl was put into a factory, where she earned 6s. a week; the eldest boy got up early one morning, and offered himself to a dairyman as a boy to leave milk, and got the job, which meant work from 6 a.m. till 8 a.m., and two hours after school in the evening. Several hours on Saturday and Sunday completed the week's work, for which he was paid 2s. 6d. His parents were averse to his doing this, but the boy persisted. The family moved to basement rooms at a cheaper rent, and then the gradual pulling down of the baby began. The mother applied to the school authorities to have the two boys given dinner, and after some difficulty succeeded. The elder boy made no complaint, but the short-legged one could not eat the meals supplied. He said they were greasy, and made him feel sick. He used to come home and ask for a slice of the family bread and dripping. The father's earnings ranged between 5s. and 10s., which brought the family income up to anything from 13s. 6d. to 18s. 6d. The food allowance went often as low as 8d. a week. A strain was put upon the health of each child, which reduced its vitality, and gave free play to disease tendencies. The eyes, which had been a weak point in every child, grew worse all round. The consumptive girl was constantly at home through illness, the boy had heavy colds, and the younger children ailed. Work was at last found by the father at a steady rate of 20s. a week. He took the consumptive girl from her work, and sent her into the country, where she remained in the cottage of a grandparent earning nothing. The boy was induced to give up his work, and the family, when last seen, were living on a food allowance of 1s. 6d. per head all round the family. The baby was the usual feeble child of her age, the children were no longer fed at school, and the parents were congratulating themselves on their wonderful good fortune.

Mr. B., whose home was visited part of 1911 and all 1912, was a printer's labourer, and brought his wife 28s. a week every week during the investigation. He had been in the army, and fought all through the South African War. He seemed to be a strong man. His wife was one of the few fairly tall women that were visited. She had been strong, but was worn out and very dreary. There were eight children, all undersized, and increasingly so as they went down the family. The ex-baby was a shrimp of a boy, only eleven months old when the baby—another boy —was born. The third youngest was a girl, and was so delicate that neither parent had expected to rear her. She weighed less than many a child of a year old when she was two and a half. The chief characteristics of these three youngest children were restlessness, diminutiveness, and a kind of elfin quickness. The baby, which was a normal child weighing 7 lbs. at birth, caught the inevitable measles and whooping - cough at four months and six months, and at a year weighed just 15 lbs. He could say words and scramble about in an extremely active way—so much so that his harassed mother had to tie him into the high chair at an earlier age than most children of his class. The eyes of all the children in this family needed daily attention, and showed great weakness. The eldest girl was supplied with spectacles at school, for the payment of which 2d. a week appeared for months in the mother's budgets. There was no specific disease. The children were stunted by sheer force of circumstances, not, so far as could be ascertained, by heredity. The sleeping was extremely crowded, and the food allowance averaged 1s. 2½d. a week, or 2d. a day for the mother and children.

A third family is interesting for the reason that the mother firmly believed in enough to eat, and, being a particularly hard-working, clean woman, she could not bear to take dark underground rooms or to squeeze her family of seven children into a couple of rooms. She solved her problem by becoming a tenant of the Duchy of Cornwall estate. She got four tiny rooms for 8s., and kept them spotless. Her husband, who was a painter's labourer and a devoted gardener, kept the tiny strip of yard gay with flowers, and kept the interior of the damp, ill-contrived little house fresh with " licks of paint " of motley colours and patches and odds and ends of a medley of papers. When work was slack, Mrs. C. simply did not pay the rent at all. As she said: " The Prince er Wales, 'e don't want our little bits of sticks, and 'e won't sell us up if we keeps the place a credit to 'im." She seemed to be right, for they owed a great deal of rent, and were never threatened with ejection. She explained the principle on which she worked as follows: " Me and my young man we keeps the place nice, and wen 'e's in work we pays the rent. Wen 'e's out er work in the winter I gets twenty loaves and 2 lbs. er sixpenny fer the children, and a snack er meat fer 'im, and then I begins ter think about payin' th' agent out er anythink I 'as left. I'd be tellin' a lie if I said I didn't owe a bit in the rent-book, and now and agen th' agent gets a shillin' er two extra fer back money, but 'e carn't 'elp seein' 'ow creditable the place is. That piece er blue paper looks a fair treat through the winder, so 'e don't make no fuss." The house they lived in, and many like it, have been demolished, and a number of well-built houses are appearing in their stead. The Lambeth people declare that the rents have gone up, however, and that the displaced tenants will not be able to return, but this rumour has not been inquired into. What happened to the C.'s overdraft when they were obliged to turn out is not known. The children of this family were short and stumpy, but of solid build, and certainly had more vigour and staying-power than those of the two other families already mentioned in this chapter. The baby flourished. She weighed 7 lbs. at birth, and at one year she weighed 18 lbs. 10 ozs. She could drag herself up by a chair, and say many words. The system of feeding first and paying rent afterwards seemed to be justified as far as the children were concerned.

Another woman who lived in " the Duchy," as they all call it, and whose house has since been demolished, had not the temperament which had the courage to owe. She paid her 8s. for rent with clockwork regularity, and fed her husband and four children and herself on a weekly average of 8s. 6d. a week. The average for herself and the children worked out at 1s. a week, or less than 2d. a day. All four children were very delicate. The baby, who weighed 8½ lbs. at birth, weighed 16 lbs. 8 ozs. at one year. The ex-baby suffered from consumption of the bowels, and was constantly in and out of hospital. The two elder children were tuberculous. The father was a printer's labourer, and appeared to be fairly strong, though a small man. The mother was delicate and worn, but seemed to have no specific disease.

Some of the children in the different families had strong individuality. Emma, aged ten, stood about 4 feet 6 inches in her socks. Four years later, when she began to earn by carrying men's dinners backwards and forwards to them at work, she measured 4 feet 10 inches. At ten she was a queer little figure, the eldest of six, with a baby always in her arms out of school-hours. She was not highly intelligent, but had a soothing way with children. Her short neck and large face gave the impression of something dwarf-like. But she was sturdy and tough to all appearance, and could scrub a floor or wring out a tubful of clothes in a masterly way. She had a dog-like devotion for a half deaf, half blind little mother, who nevertheless managed to keep two rooms, a husband, and six children in a state of extraordinary order, considering all things. When Emma's school shoes were worn out, her mother took them over and wore them till there was no sole left, and Emma was pro-vided with a " new " fifth-hand pair, which were generally twice too big. Emma's mother found her a great comfort, and very reluctantly sent her to work in a factory at the age of fifteen. There she earned 6s. a week, and became the family bread-winner during the frequent illnesses of her father.

Lulu was ex-baby to the deserted wife, and was three years old when her mother was visited. She was a lovely child with brilliant dark eyes and an olive skin. She had round cheeks, which never seemed to lose their contour, though their poor little owner spent many weary weeks in hospital after four different operations for a disease which the visitor only knew by the name of " intersections," pronounced by Lulu's mother with awe and respect. Lulu would be playing, and suddenly she would be seized with violent pain and be hurried off in her mother's arms to the hospital. The visitor was present on one of these occasions, when it seemed as though the whole street knew exactly what to do. One neighbour accompanied the mother and child, one took over the baby, another arranged with a nod and a word to take the mother's place at work that afternoon, and in two minutes everything was settled. Lulu came out of hospital four weeks later, with pale but still round cheeks and a questioning look in her eyes which gave a pathetic touch to the baby face. She still lives— the very idol of her mother—to whom the two boys are as nothing in comparison.

Dorothy, a person of two and another ex-baby, was devoured with a desire to accompany her elder brothers and sisters to school. She was a fair, thin child, with bright blue-grey eyes and straight, wispy tow-coloured hair. Her tiny body was seething with restlessness and activity. She spent her days in a high chair, from which place she twice a day shrieked and wailed a protest when the elder, happier ones started for school. She was quick as a needle, and could spend hours " writing pictures " on a piece of paper with a hard, scratchy lead pencil. She had no appetite, and had to be coaxed to eat by promises, rarely fulfilled, of taking her for a walk as soon as mother's work was done. She slept in the chair during the day, as her mother declared it was not safe to have her up stairs on the bed or she would be out the window or down the stairs directly she woke. She simply hated the baby, another girl, which had condemned her to second place and comparative neglect. At three, she was kindly allowed a place in a school near by, and her health visibly improved from that moment. She became almost pretty.

'Erbie was of an inquiring turn, and during fifteen months' visiting had at different times managed to mangle his thumb, fall into the mud of the river at low tide, and get lost for ten hours, and be returned by the police. He was excessively sorry for himself, on each occasion, while his diminutive mother took the catastrophies with infinite calm. He was eight years old and a " good scholar." Physically he was a small nondescript person, thin, and fair, and colourless, with neat features and a shrill voice, which penetrated into the core of the brain.

Joey had a tragedy attached to him, which clouded a portion of his days. He was guilty of telling a " boomer " to his parents. He said that he had been moved out of the infant school into the boys' school when he hadn't. One day his mother accompanied him to the school gate because it was raining, and she was protecting him with the family umbrella. Then the horrid truth was discovered, as the entrance for boys

is in a different street to that for infants. Joey
urgently declared that he had only been " kidding " his parents, and that when they were so
wildly delighted and took his news so seriously
he had not had the courage to tell them it was
" kidding." The net result was gloom and
disgrace, which floated round Joey's miserable
head for many days. In the middle of this awful
time he *was* moved, and the strained atmosphere
was consequently relieved. He distinguished himself in his new class, however, by his answer to a
question his teacher put to him as to the origin of
Christmas Day. " You get a bigger bit of meat
on yer plate than ever you seen before," he
replied, and after a pause he added, " and w'en
'E dies you gets a bun." The teacher had called
round to complain of this way of looking at
things, and Joey was in deep disgrace again. He
was a nice, chubby thing, with earnest ways and
some imagination. His " boomer " preyed on
him, and made him thin and anxious till the
climax was over. The second offence worried
him not at all. He was the pride and delight of
two very simple and devoted parents. His two
little sisters, both younger than himself, were
extremely attached to him.

Benny was twelve and very, very serious. He
was the boy who, without telling a soul of his plan,
offered himself to the milkman as a boy who would
leave milk on doorsteps. He earned 2s. 6d. a week
for the job, and faithfully performed the duties for

some weeks, till a man who kept a vegetable shop offered him the same money for hours which suited him better, and he changed his trade. He was a very small boy for his age, and had a grave, thin face with inflamed eyes. An over-coat, presented because the visitor could not bear to think of his doing his round in the rain and sitting all day at school afterwards in his wet clothes gave him the keenest flash of plea-sure he had ever felt. He turned scarlet and then went white. He had a resolute mouth and a quiet voice and no constitution.

There is one little picture which must be de-scribed, though the child and its mother were unknown. The visitor in Lambeth Walk met a thin, decent woman carrying a pot of mignonette. By her side, a boy about seven years old was hopping along with a crutch under one arm. His other arm encircled a pot in which was a lovely blooming fuchsia, whose flowers swung to his movements. The woman was looking straight ahead with grave, preoccupied eyes, not heeding the child. His whole expression was one of such glorified beatitude that the onlooker, arrested by it, could only feel a pang of sharpest envy. They went on their way with their flowers, and round the next corner the visitor had to struggle through a deeply interested crowd, who were watching a man being taken to prison.

Questions are often asked as to how these children amuse themselves. They are popularly supposed to spend their time at picture palaces. As far as close observation could discover, they seemed to spend their play-time—the boys shrilly shouting and running in the streets, and the girls minding the baby and looking on. They played a kind of hop-scotch marked out in chalk, which reminded the visitor of a game much beloved by her in extreme youth. Boys whose parents were able to afford the luxury seemed to spend hours on one roller skate, and seemed to do positive marvels when the nature of the roadway and the nature of the skate are considered. Girls sometimes pooled their babies and did a little skipping, shouting severe orders as they did so to the unhappy infants. One party of soldiers, whose uniform was a piece of white tape round the arm and a piece of stick held over the shoulder as a weapon, marched up and down a narrow street for hours on the first day of the August holidays, making such a noise of battle and sudden death that the long-suffering mothers inside the houses occasionally left their work to scream to them to be quiet. The pathways were full of hatless girls and babies, who looked on with interest and envy. Needless to state, no notice was taken of the mothers' remonstrance. The best game of all is an ambulance, but that needs properties, which take some finding. A box on wheels, primarily intended for a baby's perambulator, and with the baby inside, makes a wonderful sort of toboggan along the paved path. The boy sits on one corner and holds with both hands on to the edges, the baby occupies the centre, and off they go, propelled by vigorous kicks.

In holiday-time elder brothers or sisters sometimes organise a party to Kennington Park or one of the open spaces near by, and the grass becomes a shrieking mass of children, from twelve or thirteen years of age downwards. The weary mother gives them bread and margarine in a piece of newspaper, and there is always a fountain from which they can drink. When they come home in the evening, something more solid is added to their usual tea. On Bank Holiday these children are taken by their parents to the nearest park. The father strolls off, the mother and children sit on the grass. Nobody talks. There is scolding and crying and laughing and shouting, and there is dreary staring silence—never conversation.

Indoors there are no amusements. There are no books and no games, nor any place to play the games should they exist. Wet holidays mean quarrelling and mischief, and a distracted mother. Every woman sighs when holidays begin. Boys and girls who earn money probably spend some of it on picture palaces; but the dependent children of parents in steady work at a low wage are not able to visit these fascinating places—much as they would like to. Two instances of " picktur show, 2d." appeared in the budgets. One was that of a young, newly married couple. The visitor smilingly hoped that they had enjoyed themselves. " 'E treated me," said the young wife proudly. " Then why does it come in your budget ?" asked the visitor. The girl stared. " Oh, I *paid*," she explained; " he let me take 'im." The other case was that of two middle-aged people, of about thirty, where there were four children. A sister-in-law minded the children, they took the baby with them, and earnestly enjoyed the representation of a motor-car touring through the stars, and of the chase and capture of a murderer by a most intelligent boy, " not bigger than Alfie." Here again the wife paid.

The outstanding fact about the children was not their stupidity nor their lack of beauty— they were neither stupid nor ugly—it was their puny size and damaged health. On the whole, the health of those who lived upstairs was less bad than that of those who lived on the ground-floor, and decidedly less bad than that of those who lived in basements. Overcrowding in a first-floor room did not seem as deadly as over-crowding on the floor below. It is difficult to separate causes. Whether the superior health enjoyed by a first baby is due to more food, or to less overcrowding, or to less exposure to infection, is impossible to determine; perhaps it would be safe to say that it is due to all three, but whatever the exact causes are which produce in each case the sickly children so common in these households, the all-embracing one is poverty. The proportion of the infantile death-rate of Hampstead to that of Hoxton—something like 18 to 140—proves this to be a fact. The 42 families already investigated in this inquiry have had altogether 201 children, but 18 of these were either born dead or died within a few hours. Of the remaining 183 children of all ages, ranging from a week up to sixteen or seventeen years, 39 had died, or over one-fifth. Out of the 144 survivors 5 were actually deficient, while many were slow in intellect or unduly excitable. Those among them who were born during the investigation were, with one exception, normal, cosy, healthy babies, with good appetites, who slept and fed in the usual way. They did not, however, in spite of special efforts made on their behalf, fulfil their first promise. At one year of age their environment had put its mark upon them. Though superior to babies of their class, who had not had special nourishment and care, they were vastly inferior to children of a better class who, though no finer or healthier at birth, had enjoyed proper conditions, and could therefore develop on sound and hygienic lines.

CHAPTER XIV

THE PEOPLE WHO ARE OUT OF WORK

THERE is a large class of people who get less than
18s. a week, because they get irregular work.
There is also a class of people who get a regular
wage which does not rise above 18s. They
get 14s., or 15s., and are generally supposed to
be doing a boy's job. Men sometimes answer an
advertisement for a boy's place and take it
rather then go unemployed altogether. The
firms who pay by the day often have men receiving 3s. or 3s. 6d. a day and doing three days
a week. In many ways it is possible for a man
to get less than 18s. a week. He need not be
a drunkard or a slacker. He may have been ill
and lost his regular job. His employer may
have sold the business. The works on which
he was employed may suddenly finish. He
finds himself out of work and, having no money
in hand, he is forced to take anything he can get
in order to keep his children from the workhouse.
It has been possible to follow the fortunes of a
certain number of cases who, for one or other of
these reasons, fell out of work. Their subsequent
struggles afford material with which to probe
the mystery of how such people manage.

Mr. Q., a carter out of work through illness, got an odd job once or twice in the week. His wages had been 24s. Six children were born, of whom five were alive.

July 7, 1910, *had earned* 5s. 5d.			Leaving for Food, 4s. 3½d.		
	s.	d.		s.	d.
Rent ..	goes	unpaid	9 loaves	2	0¾
Insurance	lapsed		Meat	0	9
Coal	0	2	Potatoes	0	3
Soap, soda ..	0	4	Vegetables ..	0	1
Gas	0	6	Margarine ..	0	1¾
Matches	0	1	3 ozs. tea ..	0	3
Blacklead ..	0	0½	Tinned milk ..	none	
			1½ lbs. sugar ..	0	3
	1	1½	Dripping	0	6
				4	3½

Or an average per head for food of 7¼d. a week, or 1d. a day.

July 14, *had earned* 15s. 10d.			Leaving for Food, 3s. 10d.		
	s.	d.		s.	d.
Rent (two weeks)	11	0	7 loaves	1	7¼
Insurance	lapsed		Meat	0	6
Coal	0	2	Potatoes	0	3½
Gas	0	5	Vegetables ..	0	1
Soap, soda, blue..	0	4½	Margarine ..	—	
Wood	0	0½	4 ozs. tea ..	0	4
			Tinned milk ..	—	
	12	0	1½ lbs. sugar ..	0	3
			Dripping	0	6
			1 lb. jam	0	3¼
				3	10

Or an average per head for food of 6½d. a week, or less than 1d. a day.

Mr. I., bottle washer, out of work through ill-

ness, wife earned what she could. Wages 18s.
when in work.   One child born, one alive.

August 10, 1910, Mrs. I. had earned 2s. 6d.

Rent ..	..	..	..	Went unpaid.
Insurance	..	..	..	Lapsed.
Coal ◾	..	..	..	—
Lamp oil	..	..	..	—
Soap, soda	..	..	..	—

Nothing.

Mrs. I. was told by infirmary doctor to feed
her husband up.

					s.	d.
3 loaves	..	..	..	..	0	8¼
Meat ..	..	..	..	..	1	1
Potatoes	..	..	..	..	0	3
Vegetables	..	..	..	..	0	0¾
3 ozs. tea	..	..	..	..	0	3
1 lb. sugar	..	..	..	..	0	2

	s.	d.
	2	6

Average per head for food 10d., or 1½d. a day.

August 17, Mrs. I. had earned 3s. 6d.

					s.	d.
Rent ..	..	..	..	Went unpaid.		
Insurance	..	..	..		—	
Coal ..	..	..	..		0	4
Lamp oil	..	..	..	..	0	2
Soap ..	..	..	..		0	2
Firewood	..	..	..	..	0	1

	s.	d.
	0	9

Mrs. I. still feeding her husband up.

					s.	d.
4 loaves	..	..	..	..	0	11
Meat ..	..	..	..	..	1	0
Potatoes	..	..	..	..	0	2
Vegetables	..	..	..	..	0	1
1 oz. tea	..	..	..	..	0	1
1½ lbs. sugar ..	..	..	..	0	3
Margarine	..	..	..	..	0	3

	s.	d.
	2	9

Average per head for food 11d., or 1⅟₂d. per day.

When Mr. I. could earn again, his back rent amounted to 15s. He found work in the north of London, he living south of Kennington Park. He walked to and from his work every day, refusing to move because he and his wife were known in Kennington, and rather than see them go into the " house," their friends would help them through a bad spell.

Mr. J., carter out of work through illness, took out an organ when well enough to push it. Wages 18s. when in work. Six children born, six alive.

> January 26, 1910, Mr. and Mrs. J. had earned between them 9s.
> February 2, 1910, Mr. and Mrs. J. had earned between them 7s.
> February 9, 1910, Mr. and Mrs. J. had earned between them 8s. 10d.
> February 16, 1910, Mr. and Mrs. J. had earned between them 9s.
> February 23, 1910, Mr. and Mrs. J. had e arned between them 7s. 6d.

	Jan. 26.		Feb. 2.		Feb. 9.		Feb. 16.		Feb. 23.	
	s.	d.	s.	d.	s.	d.	s.	d.	s.	d.
Rent	5	6	3	0	5	6	5	6	3	6
Coal	0	6	0	6	0	4	0	6	0	6
Wood	0	1	0	1	0	1	0	1	0	1½
Lamp oil ..	0	1	0	1	0	1	0	1	0	1½
Soap, soda ..	0	2	0	2	0	2	0	2	0	4
	6	4	3	10	6	2	6	4	4	7
Leaving for food	2	8	3	2	2	8	2	8	2	11
Average for food per head a week in holidays ..	0	4	almost 5d.		0	4	0	4	0	4½

Those children who were of school age in these three families were fed once a day for five days a week during term-time. None of the children were earning. The three women were extremely clean, and, as far as their wretched means would allow, were good managers. It is impossible to lay out to advantage money which comes in spasmodically and belated, so that some urgent need must be attended to with each penny as it is earned. After a certain point of starvation food must come first, though before that point is reached it is extraordinary how often rent seems to be made a first charge on wages.

Mr. V. worked for a relative who was in business in a very small way. For driving a little one-horse cart his usual wage was only 18s., and when the business fell off Mr. V. found himself getting three days a week instead of six. Later on he got half days and odd days, which only produced a few shillings all told. He tried on off days to get odd jobs of any sort. Four children had been born, of whom two were living.

January 12, 1910, to January 19, he earned 8s. 2½d.

					s.	d.
Rent (one room at a weekly rental of 3s. 9d.) ..	..	..	..	..	2	9
Coal ..	..	..	..	..	1	4
Wood	..	..	..	..	0	1
Lamp oil	..	..	..	..	0	3
Soap, soda ..	..	..	..	..	0	2
					4	7

Leaving 3s. 7½d. for food, which is nearly 11d. a head per week, or 1½d. a day all round the family.

Between January 19 and 26 Mr. V. earned 4s. 8d.

					s.	d.
Rent ..	..	..	..	..	2	3
Coal ..	..	..	..	..	0	6
Wood	..	..	..	..	0	1
Lamp oil	..	..	..	..	0	1½
Soap, soda	..	..	..	..	0	1½
					3	1

Leaving 1s. 7d. for food.

Friendly neighbours gave a little bread and Mr. V. had some meals at a cabman's shelter in return for calling drivers when fares wanted them.

On January 27 he opened the cab-door for a lady, who gave him 2d. The police were watching him and he was arrested for begging. The visitor was enabled to see the charge sheet and speak in his favour. He was a week on remand, and three days in prison. His wife borrowed 5s. from sympathetic neighbours.

					s.	d.
Rent (of which 2s. 6d. was back rent)					3	9
Wood	..	..	..	..	0	1
Coal ..	..	..	..	..	0	4
					4	2

Leaving 10d. for food for three people. Again neighbours came to the rescue, and Mrs. V. received broken bread and several cups of tea. She spent the 10d. thus:

					s.	d.
Bread..	..	..	..	..	o	7¾
Sugar ..	..	..	..	..	o	I
Butter	..	..	..	..	o	I
2 potatoes	..	..	..	..	o	o¼
					o	10

When Mr. V. came out of prison he managed
to earn 7s. 10½d.

					s.	d.
Rent ..	..	..	..	..	3	o
Coal ..	..	..	..	..	I	4
Lamp oil	..	..	..	..	o	3
Wood	..	..	..	..	o	I
Soap ..	..	..	..	..	o	1½
					4	9½

Leaving for food 3s. 1d., which gives an average
of 9¼d. per head a week, or between 1¼d. and 1½d.
a day.

The following four weeks the money earned
was 8s. 1d., 7s. 1½d., 6s. 9d., and 10s. 7d. The
averages per head a week for food were 9¼d., 8d.,
7d., and 1s. 2½d. respectively. The rent had fallen
4s. into arrears, and Mrs. V. still owed the 5s.
borrowed when her husband went to prison.

Mr. O., a carpenter working in a theatre and
earning 30s., lost his job because his foreman
quarrelled with the management and went out,
taking all his men. Mr. O. got taken on as extra
hand in another theatre and was paid 2s. a per-
formance. Out of his 14s. he allowed his wife
13s. Mrs. O., being landlady of their house, was
responsible for 16s. a week in rent. Two lodgers

paid 6s. and 4s. for two rooms and one room respectively. Three children had been born, of whom two were alive.

January 25, 1911.

	s.	d.
Rent	6	0
Coal (very cold weather)	0	8½
Burial insurance	0	7
Gas	0	6
Wood and matches	0	3
	8	0½

Leaving for food 4s. 11½d. Mr. O. had to manage on 2s. 6d. a week for food, which left his wife and the two boys just under 2s. 6d. between them, or 10d. a week each.

February 1.

	s.	d.
Rent	6	0
Coal	0	8½
Burial insurance	0	7
Gas	0	9
Soap, soda	0	2
Coke	0	2
	8	4½

Leaving for food 4s. 7½d., which meant 2s. 1½d. for the wife and children, an average for them of 8½d. a week per head, or 1¼d. a day.

February 8.

	s.	d.
Rent	6	0
Coal	0	8½
Burial insurance	0	7
Gas	1	0
Wood, matches	0	2
Soap, soda	0	3½
	8	9

Leaving for food 4s. 3d. This week Mrs. O. was prematurely confined of twins. Both died, and the case was automatically concluded. When Mrs. O. recovered she found a place as assistant " dresser " in a theatre. Her two boys were taken care of by their grandmother, and the household struggled back to something like its previous income.

Mr. U., who lost his work because his employer wound up the business, was a steady, well-educated man. He was obliged to do odd jobs between long tramps to find a fresh billet. There were five children born, all living, but very delicate. Mrs. U. had managed by dint of extraordinary and penurious thrift to save £1 19s. 8¼d. when the crash came.

July 6, 1910, money earned 23s. 7d.

	s.	d.
Rent	7	6
Burial insurance	0	7
Coal	0	7½
Gas	1	0
Soap, soda	0	4¼
Boots repaired	2	6
Hat	1	0¾
	13	7½

Mrs. U. managed to do on 22s. 9¾d., whereby she saved 9¼d. and spent 9s. 2¼d. upon food, which means an average all round the family of 1s. 3¾d. per week, or 2¼d. a day. Mr. U. took no fixed sum for his food. His wife did the best she could for him and thought it cost her about 4d. a day, but was not sure.

The savings had now mounted to £2 0s. 5½d., but the next week the amount brought in was only 12s. 7d.

July 13.

					s.	d.
Rent ..	..	..	..	..	7	6
Burial insurance	..	..	..		0	7
Soap, soda ..	..	..	..		0	3½
Blacking ..	..	..	..		0	0½
Gas (no coal)	..	..	..		1	0
					9	5

Mrs. U. managed on 17s. 6¾d. for the week, which left 8s. 1¼d. for food, or a weekly average all round the family of almost 1s. 2d., or 2d. a day, and depleted the savings to the amount of 4s. 11¾d. The reserve fund now stood at £1 15s. 5¾d.

Next week Mr. U. made 19s. 7d., but one of the children won a prize of 2s., which gives 21s. 7d.

July 20.

					s.	d.
Rent ..	..	..	..	..	7	6
Burial insurance	..	..	..		0	7
Soap, soda ..	..	..	..		0	3
Gas (still no coal)	..	..	..		1	0
Boy's boots ..	..	..	..		2	6½
					11	10½

Mrs. U. managed on £1 0s. 9d., which allowed 8s. 10½d. for food, an average all round of almost 1s. 3¼d., or just over 2d. a day. Tenpence was saved and the reserve fund went up to £1 16s. 3¾d.

July 27, 15s. 7d. was earned, and 18s. 3¼d. was spent, of which 8s. 11d. went on food, an average all round of 1s. 3¼d., or slightly over 2d. a day. The fund went down to £1 13s. 7½d.

August 3rd, 17s. 1d. was earned, and 18s. 2½d. was spent, of which 8s. 9¼d. was spent on food, an average all round of 1s. 3d., or just over 2d. a day. The fund sank to £1 12s. 6d.

August 10, only 8s. 7d. was earned and 16s. 11¾d. was spent, of which 7s. 1¼d. went on food, an average all round of 1s. 0¼d. or 1¾d. a day. The fund was reduced to £1 4s. 1¼d.

August 17, 13s. 7d. was earned, and 16s. 0½d. was spent, of which 6s. 9½d. was spent on food, an average all round of between 11½d. and 11¾d., or less than 1¾d. a day. The fund sank to £1 1s. 7¾d.

August 24, the food average all round was 10¾d., or 1½d. a day, and the fund sank to 19s. 6d.

August 31. The food average all round was just under 1s., or 1¾d. a day, and the fund sank to 17s. 11½d.

Terror of using up the fund completely kept Mrs. U. spending an average, all round the family, of under 1s. a week for many weeks, though the earnings increased again slowly, and the fund mounted by pennies and sixpences to £1 6s. 0d. Then the baby was a year old, and the case came to an end. Mr. U. eventually got work again at a very low but regular wage. During this time of unemployment two of the three children of school age were fed at school for one term. The care committee of the school to which the other child went did not consider the case bad enough, and the two who did get fed were only received after weeks of application. The mother's very virtues told against her. Her rooms were spotless, the decent furniture, the tidy clothes of better days inclined the school visitor to believe that food could be forthcoming did the mother choose.

Mrs. X., a deserted wife with three children, fell out of work owing to a dangerous illness after the birth of her baby. When she recovered sufficiently to work again, the parish relief, which she had been receiving in kind during her illness, stopped. She took in sewing and did days' washing and cleaned doorsteps.

October 11, 1911, received 5s. 6d.

	s.	d.
Rent (4s. a week)	Went unpaid.	
Coal	0	5½
Gas	0	3
Fares to work	0	1
Soap, soda, blue (she supplied her own blue and soap when she did washing)	0	4
	1	1½

FOOD.

	s.	d.
5 loaves	1	0½
Meat	0	11½
Margarine	0	4
Potatoes	0	3½
Greens	0	1
Sugar	0	2¾
Quaker oats	0	7½
Tea	0	3
Fish	0	4½
1 tin milk	0	2
Salt	0	0¼
	4	4½

The baby was receiving six quarts of milk a week from friends, so we have 4s. 4½d. left to feed three persons—an average of 1s. 5½d., or 2½d. a day.

October 18, amount received 7s. 6d.

					s.	d.
Rent ..	..	..	..	..	4	0
Gas ..	..	..	..	..	0	3
Coal ..	..	..	..	..	0	7
Matches	..	..	..	..	0	0½
Soap, soda, etc.	..	..	..		0	3
Camphorated oil (child with a cough)					0	2
					5	3½

FOOD.						
4 loaves	..	..	..	..	0	10
Sugar ..	..	..	..	..	0	2¾
Dripping	..	..	..	..	0	2
Meat ..	..	..	..	..	0	4
Potatoes	..	..	..	..	0	3
Fish ..	..	..	..	..	0	1¾
Tea ..	..	..	..	..	0	1
1 tin milk	..	..	..	..	0	2
					2	2½

We have here 2s. 2½d. left between three persons — an average of 8¾d. a week or 1¼d. a day.

November 1, 10s. was received. The rent was one week behind.

			s.	d.
Rent (two weeks; the landlady downstairs was pressing)	..		8	0
Hat and socks	..	..	0	2
Soap, soda, etc.	..	..	0	2½
			8	4½

No coal, no gas. The great bargain of hat and socks for 2d. could not be passed by.

				s.	d.
3 loaves	..	..	..	0	7½
1 tin of milk ..	..	..	..	0	1
Potatoes	..	..	..	0	2
Dripping	..	..	..	0	3
Tea ..	..	..	..	0	1
Meat ..	..	..	..	0	4
Fish ..	..	..	..	0	2
Onions	..	..	..	0	2
Sugar ..	..	..	..	0	2
Salt and pepper	..	..	..	0	1
				2	1½

In this instance we have 2s. 1½d. to divide between three persons—an average of 8½d. a week, or 1¼d. a day.

This woman eventually became an office cleaner at 12s. a week, and her case is referred to in a previous chapter.

However steady a man may be, however good a worker, he is never exempt from the fear of losing his job from ill-health or from other causes which are out of his control. His difficulty in getting into new work is often very great, because new work in his own trade requires time and patience to find. He may have to tramp from one place of business to another day after day, and week after week. His trouble is that if he spends the whole of his time doing this no money is coming in, and he and his must live. He is therefore forced to take odd jobs which bring in something, but which spoil his chances of regular work. Numbers of men who have a

trade lose it, because they cannot afford the time
necessary to find a new job of the same kind as
the one they have lost.   They are forced to take
anything that turns up in order to keep afloat
at all.   So the friendly foreman who says, " You
turn up every morning at seven o'clock, and I'll
call for you when I want a hand," finds when he
does call several days later that the man is not
there.   No amount of explaining next day that in
order to keep his family he did a day's work
unloading a barge or sweeping snow is of avail
against the fact that another man has got the
job.   Meantime, his clothes and his very muscles
are depreciating, and work in his own trade
becomes almost an impossibility to find.   In
some employments, where it is a common custom
to give a man two, or three, or four days' work
a week and pay him by the day, it is demanded
that he should turn up every day of the week
and wait for his work, or lose the few days he has
the chance of getting.   The carters in certain
well-known West End firms are employed on
these terms.   In many employments there are
a number of extra men who take duty when the
regular man has a holiday or fails to appear.
These extra men live a life of great poverty and
great uncertainty.   The work they do may be
skilled, and they are bound to keep their hand
in, and bound to appear daily in order to secure
a few days a week for a wage which would be

barely sufficient did they get six full days.   The lives of the children of the poor are shortened, and the bodies of the children of the poor are stunted and starved on a low wage.   And to the insufficiency of a low wage is added the horror that it is never secure.

CHAPTER XV

THE STANDARD OF COMFORT

In his book, " The Living Wage," published in 1912, Mr. Philip Snowden devotes the third chapter to an estimation of the number of adult men, employed in the principal trades of the United Kingdom, who are getting less than 25s. a week. He quotes Professor Bowley, who in 1911 announced that 2,500,000 adult men were getting less than 25s. a week when working full time. This number, he explains, would be considerably increased were the figures based on actual earnings, as in almost every trade men occasionally, or even habitually, work short weeks, and get short pay during some part of the year.

Mr. Snowden, moreover, considers that Professor Bowley had under-estimated the number of adult men who, at full rates of pay, were earning less than 25s. a week. He takes Board of Trade returns, which show that in the cotton industry, which is one of the best paid of our great trades, 40 per cent. of adult men earned less than 25s. a week; that in the wool-combing industry the average wage for adult men on full time was

17s. 6d. a week; that in the linen industry 44 per cent. of the adult men earned less than 20s. a week, and 36 per cent. earned between 20s. and 30s.; that in the jute industry 49 per cent. of the adult men earned less than 20s. a week, and 36 per cent. earned between 20s. and 30s.; that in the silk industry 19 per cent. of the adult men earned less than 20s. a week, and 54 per cent. earned between 20s. and 30s.; and he took also a summary of the *actual* earnings of the adult men in the textile trades of the United Kingdom, which shows that for one week of September, 1906, 48 per cent. earned less than 25s. a week.

For other occupations, Mr. Snowden, still quoting Board of Trade figures, says that in the clothing trade 7 per cent. of adult men earned less than 20s. a week, and 27 per cent. between 20s. and 30s.

> Of bricklayers' labourers 55·9 per cent. earned under 25s. a week.
> Of masons' labourers 67 per cent. earned under 25s. a week.
> Of plumbers' labourers 54 per cent. earned under 25s. a week.
> Of painters' labourers 33 per cent. earned under 25s. a week.
> Of builders' labourers 51 per cent. earned under 25s. a week.

A still later return of the Board of Trade gives information as to the wages of railway men in 1911. The figures show that 63 per cent. of the adult men got less than 25s. a week. The earnings of agricultural labourers, as given by the Board

of Trade, for 1907 were 15s. 2d. a week in cash, or
18s. 4d. a week, counting all allowances. Mr.
Snowden sums up the clearly set out facts given
in his chapter thus:

" The facts cited in this chapter show that on
the average something like one-half of the adult
men, most of whom have a family dependent
upon their earnings, do not earn 25s. 9d. a week,
and that of this half, a very considerable proportion receive very much less than a pound a
week. When we have considered the cost of
living, it will be seen how wholly inadequate
these wages are, and how inevitable it is that the
consequences of this insufficiency should show
themselves in the physical and social conditions
of the wage-earning classes."

In his estimate, Professor Bowley calculated
that about 8,000,000 adult men were employed
in regular occupations in the United Kingdom,
and that of these 32 per cent., or nearly one-third,
were earning, at full-time work, less than 25s.
a week. As we see, Mr. Snowden comes to a
different conclusion, and reckons that 50 per cent.
of the adult men in regular employment are
getting less than 25s. a week. If we take the
smaller of these two estimates and reckon that
one-fifth of the adult men are unmarried, we get
something like 2,000,000 families living on a
wage which is under 25s. a week. Again, to
quote from Mr. Snowden, " Sir Robert Giffen
estimated twenty years ago that there were

2,000,000 families where the total income did not exceed a pound a week." Allowing that the average family consists of a man and his wife and two children, we get 8,000,000 persons who are living more or less as are the people whose daily life has been described in the previous chapters of this book, while, if we take Mr. Snowden's own estimate, the number is far greater. That means that the great bulk of this enormous mass of people are under-fed, under-housed, and insufficiently clothed. The children among them suffer more than the adults. Their growth is stunted, their mental powers are cramped, their health is undermined.

A hundred years ago their fathers would have regarded these children as economic assets, and the family income would have been produced by every member who was over a very tender age. During the last century the State prohibited the employment of children under a certain age—an age which, as wisdom grows, tends to become higher and higher. By this necessary action the State formally invested itself with the ultimate responsibility for the lives and welfare of its children, and the guardianship thus exercised has continually been enlarged in scope until it has assumed supreme control of the nurture and training of the youth of the nation. A birth now means that a new human being must be fed, clothed, and housed in a manner which the State as guardian considers sufficient, for a period which we now hope to raise to sixteen years. If a man in these days sets his young children to earn money, or, if they be not fed, clothed, cared for, and sent regularly to school, he can be put in prison. If the children's mother be a wage-earner, she can also be sent to prison if her children are not sufficiently cared for. Even the non-earning mother who has only what her husband chooses to give her can be imprisoned if a magistrate decide that any child-neglect is chargeable to her. It would seem reasonable to expect that when the ultimate responsibility for their welfare is undertaken by a rich and powerful State, children should at least be in receipt of sufficient food, shelter, warmth, and clothing.

Instead, however, of co-operating with parents and seeing to it that its wards are supplied with such primary necessaries, this masculine State, representing only male voters, and, until lately, chiefly those of the richer classes, has been crude and unwise in its relations with all parents guilty of the crime of poverty. With the best intentions it has piled upon them responsibilities which it has left them to cope with unaided. We still have the children of sober, industrious men and women living lives which maim and stunt them and make of them a handicap for the very State of which they are part. And we have parents whose wages are insufficient for their own needs spending themselves to perform the impossible, and, while they fail, the State—their partner in responsibility—looks the other way.

The first remedy for this state of things which springs to the mind of the social reformer is a legal minimum wage. The discussion of a minimum wage, which is at the same time to be a family wage, is exceedingly difficult. We realise that wages are not now paid on a family basis. If they were we should not have 2,500,000 adult men receiving for full-time work a sum which the writer has no hesitation in saying is less than sufficient for the proper maintenance, and that on the lowest scale, of one adult person. To pay wages in future, on an adequate family basis, to every adult worker who could possibly have helpless children dependent upon him or her would be a startlingly new departure. There are none, in fact, who advocate it. And yet if we are really attempting to solve the problem of hungry children by minimum wage legislation, we ought to aim at no less. Of course, what usually is advocated is the paying of a family wage to all adult men, while paying women an individual wage—the assumption being that women never maintain families. But we know this assumption to be untrue. Many thousands of women do maintain families, and if, through the medium of the minimum wage, their children also are to be kept in decency and comfort, the wages of women must also be on the family basis. Another difficulty in dealing with a family wage is the question of what sized family ? There is no standard either in numbers or in age. If the wage be calculated upon a wife and two children, it will not support a wife and six children. Nor if it be calculated upon three children under four will it support in equal efficiency three children of ten, eleven and thirteen. Further, if a law which would keep children at school until the age of sixteen should happily come into force, the difficulty of reckoning a minimum wage which would suit everybody would be still greater.

A third difficulty is the fact that money paid as wage for work done must, in the nature of things, belong wholly and entirely to the person who performs the work. He or she is free to devote such money to any purpose they think best, and cases are not unknown of children who do not receive even such nurture as their parents' means could allow. Many people solve these knotty points by dropping women bread-winners out of the problem, by arranging that the family consists of five persons—a man, his wife, and three children—and by assuming that every parent thinks more of his or her children's welfare than of self. By doing this, they deal with theories instead of facts.

The two sums that have been seriously discussed by such various authorities as Mr. Rowntree, Mr. Charles Booth, and the Labour party are 25s. a week and 30s. a week. Neither sum is really enough in some localities should there be more than three children, who are to be properly housed as well as properly dressed and fed. And neither sum as a hard and fast minimum, even for men only, is considered practical politics by anybody. Scientific minimum wage schemes must consider and give weight to the conditions of each trade and locality. Many decisions in the worst paid trades will follow the example of the decisions under the Trades Boards Act, and when a minimum has been arrived at it will be—though an advance on present wages—insufficient perhaps to keep in real efficiency and comfort a single adult.

Moreover, to keep the children of the nation in health and strength is too important and vital a responsibility to be placed entirely on the shoulders of one section of the community—namely, the employers of labour. It is a responsibility which should be undertaken by the only authority which is always equal to its complete fulfilment—the State.

Therefore, although any minimum wage scheme which proposes to raise the bottom wages in any trade or trades, or for any group or groups of workers, is a necessary part of legislation, and must be urgently insisted upon in any plan for social reform, no minimum wage legislation now proposed, or likely to be proposed, will deal adequately with the question of all the children of the working poor. Yet unless we do deal with all of them, and deal adequately, the problem of the nation's children goes unsolved.

Two theories are sometimes seriously brought forward as means by which the problem of hungry children could be dealt with. One is that if only the poor could be induced to cut down their families to fit their incomes there would be no problem. The other is, that if only the woman with 20s. a week knew how to spend it she could feed, lodge, and clothe her family with perfect ease. The first of these two ideas—if it ever possibly could be put into practice—would find a cure for poverty by the dying out of all the poor people. The man with 20s. and less could not even marry; the man with 25s. might perhaps marry, but could have no children; the man with 30s. might have one or two children—one is tempted to say " and so on." But the people with incomes over the income-tax level do not nowadays as a rule err on the side of too large families. Many people with the comparatively enormous sum of £10 a week hesitate to have more than one or two children. It is obvious that were the children of the poor limited according to wage there would be no corresponding advance in the size of the families of the rich. It is not only that the nation would shrink, but the wage-earner would automatically cease to reproduce himself. It seems an heroic way of curing his difficulties. Obviously as a palliative in individual cases the plan of limiting the family according to wage appeals with great force to the well-fed and more fortunate observer, but as a national measure to deal with poverty it fails to convince. That a man with 24s. a week is unwise to have six children is perfectly true. But, then, what sized family would he be wise to have ? If he were really prudent and careful of his future he would, on such a wage, neither marry nor have children at all. He could in that case live economically on 20s. a week and save the 4s. towards his old age. But we cannot expect Professor Bowley's 2,500,000 adult men to act on those lines. The fact is they want to marry and they want to have children. As either of these courses is unwise on 24s. a week, they are in for a life of imprudence anyhow. The very facts of their poverty—close quarters and lack of mental interest and amusement, and, above all, lack of money—help to make the limitation of their family almost an impossibility to them.

The other suggestion has been already dealt with in previous chapters. It is always worth while, of course, to teach an improvident and stupid woman to be careful and clever—if you can. But to put down all the miseries and crying wants of the children of the poor to the ignorance and improvidence of their mothers is merely to salve an uneasy conscience by blaming someone else. It is almost better to face the position and say, " The poor should not be allowed to have children," than to pretend that they could house, clothe, and feed them very well on the money at their disposal if they chose.

In Schedule A in the First Report of the Departmental Committee, with respect to the Poor Law Orders, a diet for a child of over two and under eight years is given, of which one day in any workhouse might be as follows :

Breakfast.—Bread, 5 ounces; fresh milk, ½ pint.

Dinner.—Roast beef, 1½ ounces; potatoes or other vegetables, 4 ounces ; fresh fruit-pudding, 6 ounces.

Supper.—Seed - cake, 4 ounces; cocoa (half milk), ½ pint.

No mother on 20s. a week could secure such food for her children. It is not supposed that the Departmental Committee appointed by the President of the Local Government Board would prescribe an extravagant diet, and it seems terrible that the children of the hard-working honest poor should be fed on a diet which is about half that prescribed as the most economical and very least that a healthy workhouse child should have. In this report it has been decreed that the workhouse child needs milk. Half of its evening and morning meals are to be of bread and milk. Further, " milk " is specially notified as meaning " new milk, whole and undiluted." If the workhouse child needs about a pint of whole and undiluted new milk a day, as well as other food such as vegetables, fruit, bread, and cocoa, so does the child outside the workhouse. No scheme of porridge and lentils will do for a child without milk, and milk is expensive. When the mother has fed the breadwinner in accordance with his tastes and with some semblance of efficiency, she has no chance of being able to afford even a half-ration of milk for her children. When she has balanced the problem of housing against that of feeding, and has decided on the wisest course open to her, she has still to put her children three and four in a bed. She cannot separate the infectious from the healthy, nor the boys from the girls. She can never choose a sanitary and healthful life. She can only choose the less of two great evils.

No teacher of domestic science, however capable, can instruct girls scientifically and in detail how adequately to house, clothe, clean, warm, light, insure, and feed a family of four or five persons on 20s. a week in London. The excellent instruction given by the L.C.C. teachers is based on budgets of £3, 35s., or of 28s. for a family of six persons. It was realised that to teach girls how to manage inadequately would be false teaching. If the scientific and trained teacher cannot solve the problem, the untrained, overburdened mother should not be criticised because she also fails. The work which she is expected to do is of supreme importance. It would be enlightened wisdom to enable her to do it.

CHAPTER XVI

THE STATE AS GUARDIAN

FROM a leading article in *The Times*, October 7, 1913:

" They (women) are resolved, we may take it, that laws and customs which do not recognise that their children are the children of the nation are behind the times and must be altered. Because they are the children of the nation, the nation owes them all the care that a mother owes to her own child. Because they are the future nation, the nation can only neglect them to its own hurt and undoing. That is a law of life which is proved up to the hilt by the bitter and humiliating experience of a large proportion of the disease and mortality and crime in our homes and hospitals and asylums and prisons. But it is a law of life which also carries with it this further truth—that the nation's children are the nation's opportunity."

What is needed is the true fulfilment of human parenthood which is a natural unforced and unforceable relation of the spirit as well as of the flesh. Money, and the efficient, skilled service it procures, can be provided from any source. But that close, personal affection and watchfulness essential to children which no other guardianship can replace can only be given by parents. Yet even parents can be thwarted and embittered by crushing toil and slavish drudgery until their natural affection is destroyed. The nation needs the active and free co-operation of fathers and mothers in the upbringing of its children, and it must enable them to do their share of the work.

At the present moment the nation, as super-guardian of its children, acts, in the case of the children of the poor, in a manner so baffling, so harassing, so contradictory, that the only feelings it induces in the minds of parents whose lives are passed in incessant toil and incessant want are exasperation, fear, and resentment.

Some painful cases show the way in which the State, as guardian of its children, uses its great power merely to punish the parent and not to protect the child. Where either father or mother is convicted and sentenced for cruelty, the child is often left helpless in the hands of a still more brutalised parent when he or she comes out of gaol. Cases exist in which a father, sentenced to hard labour for criminal assault on his own child, can again be given custody of that child on his return to work at the completion of his sentence. Punishment of the parent may be a terrible necessity; but the main object of reasoned public action should be permanently to protect and deliver the child.

A wife may be granted in public court separation from her husband for cruelty or desertion, with an order that he should pay her a weekly allowance for the support of the children of the marriage. By spending on summonses money she can ill afford, she may find it possible to get her husband sent to prison for non-payment of the allowance. But the court contents itself with punishing the father, and takes no steps to ensure the welfare of the children by enforcing payment.

A mother, the breadwinner for three young children, earned 12s. a week for work which took her from home in the early morning and again in the evening. During two daily absences, which cost her 2s. weekly in fares, she was obliged to leave her baby lying in its perambulator. The illness of an elder child brought an education officer to investigate his absence from school. The officer discovered the boy in bed with rheumatic fever, and the baby unattended. Meeting the hurrying mother as she came back from her morning's work, he indignantly informed her that it was against the law to leave a baby as hers had been left. She must in future pay a neighbour to care for it in her daily absences, or the police would interfere. She pleaded with him; in her ignorance of the ideals and methods of our English law, she explained her circumstances. He was, of course, sorry about it, but the upshot of their conversation was that by the direct action of

15

Public Authority the mother was forced to pay a neighbour to care for the baby, and the 10s. a week on which four persons were living was further diminished. Such a woman may be potentially a good parent had she any means by which she could make her good parenthood effective. But her experience of State guardianship of her children may be that Public Authority, without troubling as to whether or not fulfilment be in her power, forces further duties and responsibilities on to her shoulders in respect of those children—through the threatened medium of the police, with all the horrors of prison in the background.

Suppose the State, as co-guardian of the child, stripped off, when dealing with parents, the uniform of a police-constable with a warrant in his pocket. Suppose it approached them in some such spirit as that displayed by the Public Trustee when dealing with testators and executors. He offers advice, security, a free hand in carrying out any legal purpose, and he acts with or without other executors, as the case may require. Why should not the nation place all the information, all the security, all the help at its command at the service of its co-guardians, the .fathers and mothers ? Why should it not act frankly with them in the national interest, and help them to see that the needs of the child are supplied ?

The final responsibility for the child's welfare, the paramount authority in securing it, belong to the State.   Why not recognise the national responsibility by the definite appointment of a public Guardian who would enter upon the relation of co-guardian with the parents of every child at the registration of its birth ?

Even now fundamental parental obligations are supposed to be the same in all classes, but the well-to-do can fulfil them after a fashion without the assistance of the State, though often with much insecurity and strain.   Were there a department of Public Guardianship upon which every parent might rely for counsel and effective help, very many whose difficulty is not the actual housing and feeding of their children would be only too glad to take advantage of its advice. And even amongst the well-to-do, fathers and mothers die or lose their faculties, or are unfit, and the nation's children are the sufferers.

The appointment of a Public Guardian to co-operate with parents in all ranks of society is the only effective method, not only of preventing the national disgrace of " waste children," but of doing away with the hardships, the distrusts, the fears and the resentments caused amongst the workers by the present harsh and ill-defined exercise of national Guardianship.

It is to the collective interest of a nation that its children should flourish.   They are the future nation.   To them the State will be entrusted. To them the work, the duty, the scheme of things will be handed on.   Suppose children

were recognised to be more important than
wealth—suppose they were really put first—what
machinery have we which already deals with their
lives, their health, and their comfort ?   We have
a national system of education which we propose
to extend and elaborate, and to which we have
recently attached medical inspection, and we
have the time-honoured machinery of the home.
The children of the poor pass their lives within
the limits of these two institutions, and behind
both stands the State, which entirely regulates
one and is constantly modifying the other.

To equip the home for the vital responsibility
committed to its care, the new administrative
agency must have the power to go further than
the offering of advice and information to its fellow-
guardians, the parents. It must endow every
child who needs it with a grant sufficient to secure
it a minimum of health and comfort. Maintenance grants from the State are no new thing.
Inadequate grants are now made to the parents
of free scholars in secondary schools. What is
wanted is the extension and development of the
idea.   Based on the need of the child and limited
thereby, the grant would not become a weapon
to keep down wages. Men and women whose
children are secure are free to combine, to strike,
to take risks. Men and women who have the
entire burden of a family on their shoulders are
not really free to do so.

The State's guarantee of the necessaries of life

to every child could be fulfilled through various channels—some of them, as the feeding of school-children, already in existence. This is no suggestion for class differentiation. The scholars on the foundation of many of the great public schools, such as Eton and Winchester, are fed, as well as housed and educated, from the funds of old endowments. National school feeding, endowed from national wealth, would be an enlargement and amalgamation of systems already in being. There should be no such thing as an underfed school child: an underfed child is a disgrace and a danger to the State.

The medical inspection of school-children, extended to children of all classes, should lead to a universal system of school clinics, where the children would not only be examined, but treated. Baby clinics should be within the reach of every mother, and should be centres where doctors and nurses, at intervals to be dictated by them, would weigh and examine every child born within their district. At this moment any weighing centre, school for mothers, or baby clinic which does exist is fighting the results of bad housing, insufficient food, and miserable clothing—evils which no medical treatment can cure. Such evils would be put an end to by the State grant.

Nor would an intolerable system of inspection be necessary in order to see that the co-trustees of the State—the parents—should faithfully perform their part of the great work they are under-

taking. At every baby clinic the compulsory
attendances of a well-dressed, well-nourished,
well-cared-for child would be marked as satisfactory. No inspection needed. An unsatisfactory child would perhaps be obliged to attend
more often, or its condition might require the help
and guidance of a health visitor in the home. In
this way a merely less efficient home would easily
be distinguished from one which was impossible.
The somewhat inefficient home might be helped,
improved, and kept together, while, if the home
conditions were hopelessly bad, the public guardian would in the last resort exercise its power of
making fresh provision for the ward of the nation
in some better home.

As things now are, we have machinery by which
the State in its capacity of co-guardian coerces
the parents and urges on them duties which,
unaided, they cannot perform. Parents are to
feed, clothe, and house their children decently,
or they can be dealt with by law. But when, as
a matter of fact, it is publicly demonstrated that
millions of parents cannot do this, and that the
children are neither fed, clothed, nor housed
decently, the State, which is guardian-in-chief,
finds it convenient to look the other way, shirking
its own responsibility, but falling foul, in special
instances, of parents who have failed to comply
with the law.

The law which is supposed to exist for the purpose of protecting children, seems to exist for the

purpose of punishing parents, while doing nothing, or next to nothing, for the children. The idea still prevails among some care committees and school authorities that a " bad " parent must not be " encouraged " by feeding his children at school, and cases are known to exist where, in order to punish the parent, a hungry child is not fed. The one mistake an authority which considered the children first would not make would be that of punishing the child to spite the parent. Between Boards of Guardians, Care Committees, School Authorities, and Police, parents who are poor are baffled and puzzled and disheartened. It would be well for them to have a central authority whose first thought was the real welfare of the children of the State, and who blamed and punished parents only when it was clear that they deserved blame and punishment. That would be real, not false, " relief " of the poor.

THE END